INTRODUCTION TO ROMAN LAW

INTRODUCTION

TO

ROMAN LAW

by

Ph. J. Thomas

Professor of Roman Law
at
the University of Pretoria

Kluwer Law and Taxation Publishers
Deventer · Antwerp
London · Frankfurt · Boston · New York

Distribution in U.S.A. and Canada
Kluwer Law and Taxation
190 Old Derby Street
Hingham MA 02043 U.S.A.

Library of Congress Cataloging in Publication Data
Thomas, Ph. J.
Introduction to Roman law.

Bibliography: p. 1. Roman law. I. Title.
LAW 340.5'4 85-23646
ISBN 90-6455-245-6

D/1986/2664/8

ISBN 90 6544 2456

CONTENTS

PREFACE

Tempora muntantur et nos mutamur in illis is an appropriate motto for a book of this type. Since the *curricula* of most law schools have undergone drastic changes in the last *decennia*, the approach towards Roman law has been modified. Although the tendency towards a more practically orientated study has to be applauded, the practice of law would have most dangerous results without diligent study of theory. In order to understand something, it is necessary to return to its origin, because something is only perfect if it comprises all its relevant parts and which part is more important than the beginning. Therefore, Roman law which forms the basis of many legal systems has to be studied to lead to greater understanding. This book endeavours to present the basic principles of Roman law and a brief outline of its history, as simply and systematically as possible. Thus, no references to sources or other authorities are included, since there are many textbooks available to provide this information to the student who wishes to make an indepth study of a certain topic of Roman law.

Having stated the goal of this work I like to end by expressing my gratitude to Luanda Hawthorne and Claire Dillon for their assistance.

Ph.J. THOMAS

CHAPTER I – History

Roman law was in force (for) approximately twelve hundred years and it is, therefore, obvious, that during this period Roman law developed. Law is one of the products of a society and no society remains stagnant, but change and progress will always and everywhere take place, causing the legal system to adapt.

1. Periods

MONARCHY 753-509 BC

Legend had it that Rome was founded in 753 BC by Romulus. Be that as it may, it can be accepted that there was originally a small, agricultural community ruled by a king with virtually unlimited power.

The despotic behaviour of the last king caused the abolition of the monarchy in 509 BC.

REPUBLIC 509-27 BC

The king was replaced by two magistrates, *consules*. Gradually as Rome extended herself, other magistrates with specific functions were elected.

Furthermore, other institutions, the popular assembly and the senate, obtained more political significance. The early republican period was characterized by the internal struggle between the two classes, the patricians and plebeians, while the last two centuries of the pre-Christian era saw her establish herself as a world power. After a series of successful wars Rome became first the mistress of Italy, thereafter of the Mediterranean basin and finally of virtually the whole ancient world.

PRINCIPATE 27 BC-284 AD

The constitutional structure of the republic was not suitable to govern the world power which Rome had become and consequently a new constitutional form was introduced, the so-called principate. Augustus, the first emperor, maintained the republic in theory, but for all practical purposes, the real power was concentrated in his hands. He was leader of the senate, *princeps senatus*, and the republican institutions became tools in his hands and their influence rapidly declined. During the principate Rome attained her highest glory.

DOMINATE 284 AD
The emperor became an absolute monarch, he was *dominus et deus*, master and god.

The reorganization of the state succeeded in restoring order to a certain degree, but could not stop the decline of the Roman empire. The following centuries saw increasing pressure on the frontiers, invasion by barbaric tribes, civil war and a collapsing economy.

The empire was divided into the Western empire, with Rome as its capital, and the Eastern empire, with Constantinople as the capital. The West slowly fell prey to the invasions of Germanic tribes and the year 476 AD is traditionally accepted as the date of the fall of the Western empire, which disintegrated into several Germanic states.

The Eastern empire underwent Hellenistic and oriental influences and a new civilization with a stratified society developed.

As far as legal history is concerned, the most important period in the history of the Eastern empire was the reign of Justinian from 527-565 AD.

2. Constitutional structure

MONARCHY 735-509 BC
Knowledge of the regal period is scarce and uncertain, but it is certain that all power was in the hands of the king. He was advised by the senate, in which the heads of the aristocratic families had a seat. The existence and role of the popular assemblies is shrouded in mystery.

REPUBLIC 509-27 BC
The executive power of the erstwhile king passed into the hands of two *consules*, but later other magistracies were created to perform the executive functions.

With regard to the *magistratus* three principles applied: annuality, collegiality, liability.

Annuality meant that the *magistratus* held office for a year only.

Collegiality entailed that there were at least two *magistratus* of co-equal power in the same office.

Liability signified that a *magistratus* could be held liable for his acts in office.

The *magistratus* were elected by the popular assembly, which invested them with *imperium*, the power of the Roman people, or in the case of lesser magistracies *potestas*. From the *imperium* the magistrates derived their authority over the people and the power to promulgate edicts, the so-called *ius edicendi*, and enforce these, the so-called *coercitio*.

Coercitio took place by means of *vincula*, shackles, *verbera*, flogging, *multa*, fines, *pignoris capio*, the taking of property as security and originally the *ius gladii*, death penalty. As more magistracies were created each magistrate exercised his power in relation to his own specific function.

VARIOUS MAGISTRATUS

Two *consules*, who originally exercised all executive functions, i.e. commanding the army, administration of justice and administration of the state, were the first republican magistrates.

In 443 BC two *censores* were appointed to organize the *census*. Censors were elected every five years, but held office only for eighteen months, which was an exception to the general Roman principle of annuality.

In 367 BC the *Leges Liciniae Sextiae* introduced the magistracy of the *praetor*, which was the most important office for the development of Roman law. The *praetor*'s function was the administration of civil process, *iurisdictio*, in Rome. In 242 BC a second *praetor* magistracy was established, the *praetor peregrinus* to control litigation between *peregrini*, foreigners, or Roman and *peregrinus* in Rome.

In 367 BC the *aediles curules* were also elected for the first time. They were minor officials who supervised law and order in relation to public roads, markets etc. The administration of justice in the provinces was the responsibility of the *praeses provinciae*, the governor of the province. There were also a variety of plebeian officers, the most important of which were the *tribuni plebis*.

LEGISLATURE

The legislative power vested in theory in the popular assembly, whose principal functions were the enactment of *leges*, laws, and the election of the magistrates.

All male Roman citizens with *ius suffragii*, the vote, had a seat in these assemblies. The popular assembly met when convened by the appropriate magistrate, who would place a proposal before them. This proposal could then be approved or rejected and this was done on a block vote system, not by the method of one man, one vote.

The blocks which had a vote varied according to the subjectmatter. The voting took place either by *curia*, a unit going back to ancient times, its members connected by religious and political interest, or by *centuria*, century, or by *tribus*, tribe, but later by geographical unit.

Depending whether voting was done by *curia, centuria* or *tribus*, the assembly gathered in the following forms:

COMITIA CURIATA

There were thirty *curiae* and the most important function of this form of *comitia* was to vote on the *lex de imperio*, whereby the imperium was vested in magistrates. Twice a year it was convened as the *comitia calata* for the making of wills and *adrogatio*.

COMITIA CENTURIATA

This was the most important form of *comitia*. The voting units, the centuries did not contain a hundred people, but were constituted according to wealth, thus giving the wealthiest members of society a majority. Here the important magistrates were elected and laws enacted.

COMITIA TRIBUTA

Eventually, there were thirty five *tribus* and they elected the lesser magistrates and could enact laws.

CONCILIUM PLEBIS

During the first half of the republican period the struggle between the classes was an important factor. On the one side stood the *patricii*, the patricians, the wealthy and influential aristocrats from whose ranks the senate was constituted, the magistrates elected, the pontiffs came and who dominated the *comitia*. On the other side, stood the *plebeii* or *plebs*, the plebeians, the proletariat with no political and few social rights, who struggled for political equality.

In 494 BC the plebeians resorted to the *secessio plebis*, a secession from the city, by withdrawing to the Aventine hill, and constituted their own assembly, the *concilium plebis*. This assembly elected the plebeian officers and voted on their proposals in the same manner as the *comitia*.

SENATE

The senate comprised three hundred members, selected by the *censores*. A senator had to be thirty-one years old and was usually a former magistrate. The senate was convened by the magistrates. The functions of the senate were varied. In principle the senate was a consultative body and its main function was to advise the magistrates. The senate had, however, control of public finance, which placed magistrates whose activities entailed expenses for the state in a dependant position.

In addition, the senate had an important function in connexion with the enactment of laws.

Auctoritas patrum, ratification by the senate, as required before legislation and elections of the *comitia* became operative. This led to the practice that proposed bills and elections would be discussed in the senate before introduction in the *comitia*. Moreover, the senate conducted foreign affairs and had certain sacral functions.

The result of all this was that the *Senatus Consulta*, resolutions of the senate, which were in theory only advice, gradually acquired the force of law.

During the republican period the senate became the most powerful body and held the real leadership of the state. The reasons were twofold: firstly the yearly change of magistrates made the permanent senate the one stable body of the republic, while in the second place the popular assemblies lost their meaning as Rome extended herself and it became practically impossibly for the Romans to attend.

EMPIRE 27 BC-1453 AD

The executive power was in the hands of the emperor and his bureaucracy. The emperors introduced a new bureaucracy which gradually replaced the old republican magistracies.

The legislative power was transferred to the senate, which became an instrument of the emperor, who finally assumed legislative powers.

3. The law: period of the kings and the republic

Against the abovementioned background the development of Roman law can be discussed.

PERIOD OF THE KINGS

The early legal system of Rome was primitive, characterized by formalism, rigidity and a limited field of application.

Thus, only few legal acts were in existence. Moreover, there was no distinction between *ius*, law, and *fas*, religious rule, and the legal knowledge as well as the administration of justice was in the hands of the pontiffs.

REPUBLIC

During this period Rome extended and developed and it is obvious that the old legal system was incapable of meeting the requirements of this new society. Three factors influenced the development of Roman law during the republic, i.e. the *Lex Duodecim Tabularum*, the code of the Twelve Tables, the *praetor* and the lawyers.

As has been stated, old Roman law was formalistic, rigid and narrow; it was, moreover, exclusively applicable to Roman citizens and this system of law was called *ius civile* or *ius Quiritium*, the law of the Roman citizens. From about the third century BC the expansion of Rome brought her into the world of commerce; the Romans were compelled to make provision for relations with foreigners and this led to the notion of *ius gentium*.

Ius gentium, the law of all people, denoted certain legal principles which were in force everywhere. Thus, certain legal rules were applicable among all peoples in more or less the same form and it was these rules and principles which applied in the commercial contracts the Romans made with other people.

The *ius gentium* was characterized by informality and relied on *bona fides*, good faith, and *aequitas*, equity. The Romans named this customary law the *ius gentium* and adopted it and applied it in Roman law. In this manner Roman law developed into a legal system well-suited to answer the demands of the extremely complex and sophisticated society which Rome had become at the end of the republican period. The formalism and rigidity of the old legal system had disappeared and was replaced by good faith and equity as the main characteristics of the expanding legal system.

4. Lex duodecim tabularum

During the struggles of the patricians and the plebeians one of the complaints of the latter was that the law as well as the rules of litigation, i.e. the formal declarations and other formalities, were unknown to them, since such knowledge rested with the pontiffs, then exclusively patricians, and was guarded as religious mystery.

In 462 BC a *tribunus plebis, Terentilius Arsa*, demanded a statement of the law as well as that the law of procedure would be made public knowledge. After procrastination by the patricians a commission was sent to Greece to make a study of the code of Solon. In 452 BC the *decemviri legibus scribundis*, ten men to draw up the law, were elected. This commission was temporarily given all power in the state in order to codify the law. After an eventful two years this task was completed in 450 BC and accepted by the *comitia*. The result was inscripted on twelve tables made of wood or bronze and placed on the *forum Romanum*, the marketplace in Rome. The original tables were destroyed during the Gallic invasion of 390 BC.

THE IMPORTANCE OF THE CODE OF THE TWELVE TABLES

The Twelve Tables were the first codification of Roman law and even if the law of that period was primitive and without much material influence, the codification of the entire body of law led to the first systematic treatment of the law.

Moreover, it guaranteed security and uniformity of justice and secularized the law. Since the sentences of the Twelve Tables were brief and simple the need for interpretation arose, which was the first step towards the creation of a legal science.

Livy speaks of the Twelve Tables as the *fons omnis publici privatique iuris*, the source of all law, public and private. This is an exaggeration, but they can be said to have constituted a political victory for the *plebs* and to have laid the foundation for further legal development.

5. The praetor

The magistracy of the *praetor* was created in 367 BC by the *Leges Liciniae Sextiae.* Elected for a year by the *comitia* the *praetor*'s main function was *iurisdicto*, the administration of civil process.

It should be stressed that the *praetor* did not act as a judge, in other words he did not resolve the dispute between the parties, but saw to it that the litigants followed the correct procedure, formulated their dispute correctly and appeared before a judge.

Stricty speaking the *praetor* was not a law-giver, but as will be shown, he did become one of the main developers of new law.

The cause of the fact that the *praetor* became a chief source of law and the method he followed were as follows: As a result of his *imperium* the *praetor* had the *ius edicendi*, the power to promulgate edicts, relating to his office. In these edicts he would publish not only the process litigants had to follow, in other words the law of procedure, but also the legal remedies, such as actions and interdicts, which the *ius civile* supplied. Where the *ius civile* did not supply a remedy, the *praetor* could, on the strength of his *imperium*, introduce a new legal remedy by way of his edict. These new remedies did not only extend the old law, but introduced flexibility, good faith and equity into Roman law, since the *praetor* borrowed primarily from the *ius gentium*.

When he assumed his office, the *praetor* published his edict on the *album*, a white washed wooden tablet, on the *forum Romanum*, where he had his chair on *dies fasti*, days on which litigation could take place. His edict only remained in force for the one year of this period of office and was known as *edictum annuum* or *perpetuum*. During the year the necessity for an interim edict might arise and the *praetor* then issued an interim edict, *edictum repentinum*. Understandably, the next *praetor* usually used his predecessor's edict and made only necessary changes and additions. The fixed core of the edict, which was handed down from year to year was known as *edictum tralaticium*. Consequently, the edict showed a large degree of constancy. In 67 BC a *lex Cornelia* forbade the *praetor* to deviate from his *edictum perpetuum*, which was in practice synonym to the *edictum tralaticium*.

In 130 AD the praetorian creativity was ended by the *Edictum Perpetuum*.

As a result of the *praetor*'s activities, a new body of law, the *ius honorarium* grew, which should be distinguished from the *ius civile*.

Ius honorarium was the law which was created by the magistrates, but since the *praetor* was by far the most active source of law, it is also known as the *ius praetorium*, Magistral or praetorian law was characterized by flexibility, good faith and equity, which is not surprising, since the *praetor* drew heavily on the *ius gentium*. The *ius honorarium* was, however, not synonymous with *ius gentium*.

6. The jurists

Originally the legal knowledge was in the hands of the pontiffs, since *ius* was not distinguished from *fas*. Although the Code of the Twelve Tables and the creation of the office of the *praetor* made inroads into their monopoly, this did not destroy it.

At the beginning of the third century BC, jurists who were not pontiffs appeared.

According to legend, the first step was taken in 304 BC by *Gnaeus Flavius*, who published the formulas of ancient procedure, as well as the calendar of *dies fasti et nefasti*, the so-called *Ius Flavianum*.

A second important event took place in 252 BC, when a pontiff, *Tiberius Coruncanius*, for the first time gave legal advice and opinions in public, *publice profiteri*, which at the same time was the first teaching of law.

Finally the *Tripertita* of *Sextus Aelius Paetus Catus* should be mentioned. Published in about 200 BC this work contained three parts, i.e. the text of the Twelve Tables, an interpretation thereof and the formulas of procedure.

Gradually a body of jurists, *iurisprudentes, iurisconsulti* or *iurisperiti* emerged. They gave their advice without payment since they were wealthy and public-spirited; their reward lay in increased prestige and authority. Although representatives of the legal science, the Roman lawyers were primarily involved in legal practice.

FUNCTIONS OF THE JURIST

The functions of the jurist can be summarized as *respondere, docere, cavere, agere, interpretare* and *scribere.*

Respondere was the jurist's most important function, giving legal advice to his client. The latter may be a private person, the *praetor* or a *iudex*, a judge who was a private citizen. The *responsa prudentium*, the legal opinions of the jurists, became increasingly authorative.

Docere indicates the teaching of law. Since the *responsa* were given in public, prospective jurists were free to come to listen and learn.

Cavere denotes the safeguarding of a client's interest. The jurist advised his client with regard to formalities to be followed in legal transactions, in drawing up legal documents or instituting legal proceedings.

Agere was to give assistance in a process. The jurist would prepare the case for court, but did not appear in court himself. This task was left to the client himself or was handled by an *orator*.

Interpretare means the interpretation and application of existing legal rules and principles. The jurist applied the general rule to the individual case, but an important aspect was that the jurists extended Roman law by interpreting and applying the existing law in such a fashion, that the rule obtained a new field of application and consequently new law was created.

Finally, *scribere*, writing on the subject of law. The jurists began to write, which entailed that the body of law became systematized and a legal science developed, which remains until today, the basis of modern legal science.

Legal science as developed by the jurists reached it's zenith during the first two and a half centuries AD, the classical period which coincides more or less with the principate.

7. Sources of Roman law during the republican period

Mos, customary law, formed the basis of Roman law. The people lived according to their customs and usages and gradually it became accepted that they had to live that way, in other words that these customs were law. The *praetor* and the jurist developed the customary law.

Furthermore, there were the written sources of law, *leges, plebiscita, Senatus Consulta, Edicta* and *responsa prudentium*.

Leges, enactments of the *comitia*, were relatively insignificant in Roman private law.

Plebiscita, resolutions of the *concilium plebis*, were originally only binding on plebeians, but became generally binding in 287 BC by the *Lex Hortensia*.

Senatus Consulta, resolutions of the senate, were in theory only of an advisory nature during the republic. However, as a result of the predominant position of the senate their resolutions had force of law for all practical purposes.

Edicta, the edicts of the magistrates created *ius honorarium*.

Responsa prudentium, the opinions of the jurists were the final written source of law, specifically by way of *responsa* and *interpretatio*.

8. Roman law during the empire

During the republican period the *praetor* and the jurists developed Roman law into a legal system which could adapt to the challenges of the rapidly changing circumstances. It was during the principate that Roman law reached its highest glory, as a result of the work of the jurists and this is known as the classical period of Roman law. After this period legal science and thus Roman law declined.

The dominant factors influencing Roman law during the empire were the *praetor*, the jurists and the emperor.

THE PRAETOR

The *praetor* was a republican magistrate and gradually became subordinate to the emperor. Furthermore, the emperors created new posts which replaced the functions of the republican magistrates.

In 130 AD the emperor Hadrian commissioned the jurist *Salvius Julianus* to consolidate the edicts of the *praetor* and other magistrates into a form of code and thus was given force of law by a *Senatus Consultum*. Officers exercising jurisdiction were instructed to exercise their functions in accordance with this edict, the *Edictum Perpetuum*. This codification of the *ius honorarium* meant the end of the praetorian creativity of new law.

THE JURISTS

Two factors which contributed to the jurists attained their peak during the classical period were the *ius respondendi* and the schools of the *Sabiniani* and *Proculiani*.

The first emperor, *Augustus*, attempted to extend his control over the jurists by introducing the *ius respondendi*, the right to give legal opinions under his authority. He conferred this right on certain prominent jurists and understandably the *responsa* of these jurists enjoyed added authority. A practical consequence was that *responsa* had to be in writing and sealed from that day on, the *responsa signata*.

The emperor Hadrian solved the practical problem which arose by decreeing that if a majority of jurists with the *ius respondendi* were of the same opinion then this was binding on the judge. In all other cases a judge had a right to choose between conflicting opinions.

The schools of the Sabinians and the Proculians made their appearance in the first century AD. These schools were not places of instruction in law, but groups centred around distinguished jurists where a similar approach to the law prevailed. There existed no fundamental difference of principle between the schools, but their existence promoted discussion on legal topics and legal science benefitted from the open debate.

The *Proculiani* were founded by *Labeo*, named after *Proculus*. Illustrous members were *Nerva*, father and son, *Pegasus, Celsus*, father and son, and *Priscus*.

The *Sabiniani*, founded by Capito, were named after *Sabinus*. Among its members were *Cassius Longinus, Javolenus, Salvius Julianus, Pomponius* and *Gaius*. Although *Augustus* was careful to preserve the independance of the jurists, the leading jurists gradually became associated with the imperial government, at first as advisers, later as civil servants. This meant that they lost their independance which eventually resulted in the fact that during the dominate few prestigious jurists appeared and legal science declined.

Some celebrated jurists must be mentioned.

Sextus Aelius Paetus Catus, who wrote the *Tripertita* about 200 BC.

Marcus Tullius Cicero, the famous jurist and orator who lived towards the end of the republican period.

Gaius who lived during the second century AC, was not one of the prestigous jurists, but rather a teacher of law. He did not have the *ius respondendi*, but his fame rests on his *Institutiones*, a textbook for students, written in approximately 160 AD.

The importance of these Institutes is twofold. In the first place, it is the only work of a classical lawyer which has come to us almost complete and, therefore, an important source of classical law. Secondly, the Institutes were concisely written and thus became a popular textbook in the post-classical period. A post-classical adaptation, the *Epitome Gai* was used for the barbarian codes of the sixth century AD. Justinian also used the Institutes of Gaius as an example and basis for his own Institutes.

Papinianus (Papinian) murdered in 213 AD on the orders of emperor Caracalla, devoted his writings almost entirely to the casuistry of legal practice.

Paulus (Paul), early in the third century AD, wrote commentaries on the *Edictum* and on the *ius civile* etc. His most famous work is the so-called *Sententiae Pauli*, post-classical simplified version of his original, which was incorporated in a later barbarian code.

Ulpianus (Ulpian), a contemporary of Paulus, wrote commentaries on the *Edictum* as well as the *ius civile* etc. His best-known work is the so-called *Regulae Ulpiani*, a post-classical version of his institutional introduction for legal students.

Modestinus who lived during the first half of the third century was the last of the great classical jurists. The post-classical period saw the decline of Roman law and legal science.

The tendency to simplify the law culminated in the *Lex Citationis* of 426 AD. Promulgated in both the Eastern and the Western part of the empire this legislation attempted to systematize the jurisprudence, known as *ius* in those days, and to alleviate the difficulties of legal practice. The main provisions of this enactment were that in future only the works of the five great jurists, *Paulus, Papinianus, Gaius, Ulpianus* and *Modestinus*, were authorative. These works were to be used by way of counting of heads, namely the opinion of the majority was binding on the courts. If there was no majority opinion, the view of *Papinianus* was to be followed and only if *Papinianus* was silent, could the judge use his own discretion. In exceptional cases the works of other jurists could be consulted.

Evidence of the lowering of the standard in the post-classical period was the popularity of abridgments and simplified versions of the works of the classical jurists, for example the *Epitome Gai, Sententiae Pauli* and *Regulae Ulpiani*.

9. The emperor and the law

Immediately after the end of the republic, the emperor began to play an important role in Roman law. Originally his influence manifested itself indirectly by manipulation of the old republican institutions, but as the old republic was gradually dismanted, the emperor became the only source of law, since not only the legislation but also the administration of justice rested firmly in his hands.

LEGISLATION DURING THE EMPIRE

Although in theory the legislative power during the principate was in the hands of the senate, the predominance of the emperor in the senate made this institution an instrument of the emperor, with the result that the emperor came to be regarded as the real source of law. The emperor increasingly manifested his legislative will directly in other ways, causing the *Senatur Consulta* to disappear as a source of law towards the end of the principate.

The foundation of the emperor's legislative power was obscure and is not found in legal explanation, but in political reality. The power of the emperor was such, that nobody dared question his assumption of the legislation.

The explanations of *Gaius* and *Ulpianus* that the power to legislate was conferred on the emperor by *lex regia* or *lex de imperio* were, therefore, incorrect.

The emperor's power is aptly explained in the adagia, *Quod principi placuit, legis habet vigorem*, the emperor's will is as good as a statute, and *princeps legibus solutus est*, the emperor is not bound by statutes.

The forms in which the emperor manifested his will were many and were covered by the general term *constitutio*. In later law the *constitutiones* were also described as *leges* in contrast with *ius*, in the sense of jurisprudence.

VARIOUS MANIFESTATIONS OF CONSTITUTIONES

Edicta, edicts. In the same way as any magistrate with *imperium*, the emperor had the *ius edicendi*. His *ius edicendi* was, however, lifelong and not restricted to a specific office. His edicts were thus universal and remained in force even after his death until repealed.

Decreta, were rulings of the emperor in his capacity as a judge. Although in principle only binding in the particular case, the *decreta* were in practice regarded as statements of the law, binding in subsequent cases and a doctrine of judicial precedent evolved.

Rescripta were written answers made by the emperor to petitions of law by his officials or private persons. In the former case the *rescriptum* was in the form of an *epistula*, a separate letter, while in the latter case it took the form of a *subscriptio*, an appendage to the original petition.

Mandata were directions of the emperor to his officials. Although administrative in character, occasionally new rules of law were laid down in this manner.

As the quality of the *constitutiones* decreased through the post-classical period, the quantity increased which resulted in a chaotic mass which was of little practical use. The need for a systematic collection of the imperial legislation was consequently keenly felt and the following collections resulted.

Codex Gregorianus. A private collection, which appeared towards the end of the third century, systematized the *constitutiones* from *Hadrianus* (117-130 AD) to the reign of *Diocletianus.*

Codex Hermogenianus. A private collection of the constitutions of *Diocletianus* appeared early in the fourth century AD.

The first official collection of imperial legislation was the *Codex Theodosianus.* The product of a commision appointed by Theodosius II it was published and came into force in 438 AD. All previous imperial legislation was replaced by the *Codex Theodosianus.* This work was divided into sixteen books, each book in turn divided into *tituli*, chapters, and in each chapter the relevant constitutions with regard to a particular subject were arranged in chronological order.

10. Barbarian codifications

In 476 AD the Western Roman Empire came to an end. However, according to the principle of the personal application of laws, the Roman subjects of the Germanic kings carried on living according to Roman law. The barbarian conquerors made provision for their Roman subjects by drawing up codes.

Edictum Theodorici. This was composed and issued in the middle of the fifth century AD for *all* subjects of the western Gothic kingdom, which lay in Switzerland, south-west France and part of Spain. This code was almost entirely based on Roman law and the material for its 154 chapters was drawn mainly from the *Codices Gregorianus, Hermogenianus* and *Theodosianus*, from the *Sententiae Pauli* and the *Epitome Gai.*

Lex Romana Visigothorum or *Breviarium Alaricianum.* In 506 AD king Alaric II had a code issued for his Roman subjects. The material was drawn from the three abovementioned *Codices*, the *Sententiae Pauli, Epitome Gai* and one *responsum* of *Papinianus.*This code became an important source of law in a large part of Europe after the end of Gothic rule.

Lex Romana Burgundionum. Promulgated in about 520 AD for the Roman subjects of the Burgundian kingdom, eastern France, this code rested on the same sources as the *Lex Romana Visigothorum.*

The quality of these Germanic codes was poor and the codes were coloured by Germanic influences. Their importance is found in the information they provide on vulgar Roman law, the law of the post-classical period, in the western empire.

11. Justinian (527-565 AD)

Justinian, the emperor of the eastern Roman empire, the capital of which was Constantinople or Byzantium, attempted to restore the old glory of the Roman empire. His attempts resulted in the temporary reconquest of North Africa and Italy, his ecclesiastical policy of unifying the Church and his codification of Roman law.

In this respect Justinian aimed at restoring Roman law to the glory of the classical period and at unifying the legal system. The resulting codification preserved classical Roman law for posterity.

The inspirer of the whole project was Tribonian, the *quaestor sacri palatii*, minister for justice, who exercised significant influence throughout the whole enterprise and it is a fact that after his death in 546 AD Justinian's legal activity showed a marked decline.

COMPOSITION OF THE CODIFICATION

Codex Vetus

In 528 AD Justinian appointed a ten-man commission by the *Constitutio Haec*. The members included Tribonian and Theophilus, a law professor from Constantinople. The commission was instructed to collect all imperial constitutions, to systematize these, eradicate obsolete legislation, banish contradictions and repetitions and make, if necessary, adaptations to suit modern times. The commission made use of the existing *Codices*, with the result that the work was completed within a year. The *Constitutio Summa* gave it statutory force in 529 AD and all imperial constitutions not included went out of force. After the successful codification of the *leges* in the *Codex*, Justinian undertook the codifying of the *ius*.

Quinquaginta Decisiones. These were 50 *constitutiones* Justinian issued in 530/531 AD as a preliminary step for the codification of the *ius*.

The aim of these constitutions was to decide the conflicting opinions of the jurists and to abolish obsolete legal provisions. The *Quinquaginta Decisiones* have not survived as a collection and were probably incorporated in the later *Codex*.

THE DIGESTA

In 530 AD the *Constitutio Deo Auctore* instituted a commision of sixteen, with Tribonian as chairman, for the purpose of the codification of the jurists law.

The commision consisted of four professors of the law schools of Constantinople and Beirut, eleven practicing advocates and one imperial official. The professors formed the backbone of the commission and their inclusion facilitated the task, since the old jurisprudence was still in use at the law schools.

The commission was instructed to collect the classical legal literature, to make excerpts, to systematize these fragments, to eliminate contradictions and repetitions and if necessary adapt the old law to the requirements of contemporary practice.

Planned to take ten years, the finished result was published three years later. The most likely explanation for the speed with which the work was effected is to be found in the Massentheorie of Friedrich Bluhme. According to Bluhme the commission was divided into three sub-committees each of which dealt with a distinct group of classical writings. The first group, the *pars Sabiniana*, was formed by the *libri ad Sabinum*, classical commentaries on the *tres libri iuris civilis* by *Sabinus*. The kernel of these commentaries on the *ius civile* was the work of *Paulus, Ulpianus* and *Pomponius*.

The second group, the *pars Edictalis*, was formed by the *libri ad Edictum*, classical commentaries on the *Edictum Perpetuum*. The kernel of these commentaries on the *ius honorarium* was the work of *Ulpianus* and *Paulus*.

The third group, the *pars Papiniana*, dealt with the casuistic literature of which *Papinianus'* work formed the most important part.

Finally, there was the *Appendix* which comes from a variety of lesser-known works and was given to the committee with the Papinian mass.

Justinian reports that they worked through two thousand books containing more than three million lines.

The finished result, the *Digesta*, was divided into fifty books, which in their turn were divided into *tituli*, titles. In each title the relevant fragments regarding a specific topic are arranged. These fragments are also called *leges* and at their beginning there stands the name of the author in question and the work and book from which the excerpt has been taken.

The longer fragments or *leges* are divided into paragraphs and the first paragraph is always called the *principium*, pr, with the result that 1 is thus really the second paragraph.

The fragments were taken from the works of thirty-nine jurists, but the overwhelming majority consisted of the work of the five great jurists, *Ulpianus, Paulus, Papinianus, Gaius* and *Modestinus*. In fact four-fifths of the *Digesta* came from their works, the remaining one-fifth from the works of the other thirty-four jurists. The accent fell on the work of the classical jurists, as only three republican jurists and three post-classical jurists were included.

In 533 AD the *Constitutio Tanta*, the Digest came into force.

INTERPOLATIONES

The commission was also instructed to make changes in the text of the classical material to adapt it to contemporary requirements. These changes, called *interpolationes* or *emblemata Triboniani*, obscure the classical law and since the Digest is the principal source of classical jurisprudence, efforts were made to uncover the interpolations and thus make the pure law of the classical period accessible.

The search for interpolations originated in the sixteenth century humanism and became active since the end of the last century. It is nowadays accepted that not all contradictions and confusions in the Digest are the work of the codifying commission. The writings of the classical jurists reached the commission in a form already changed, with copying mistakes, ommissions, additions, paraphrases, explanations and illustrations.

Nevertheless, considering the speed with which the work was done weaknesses were unavoidable.

Innumerable contradictions, aggravated by Justinian's prohibition of the writing of commentaries on his legislation often lead to confusion with regard to the Justinianic law.

Institutiones

Justinian realized the importance of the study of law. He reorganized the legal education and summoned Tribonian, Theophilus and Dorotheus to publish an official textbook for beginners in the study of law. It was based on the *Institutiones* of Gaius, whose work was outdated, and the new textbook was arranged in four books, subdivided into titles, the titles arranged in paragraphs. Completed in 533 AD this book was given statutory force.

Codex repetitae praelectionis

The *Codex* of 529 AD had become outdated as a result of the subsequent codification. Tribonian, Dorotheus and three advocates were instructed to adapt the *Codex*, to eliminate obsolete constitutions and to include the new reforming constitutions, the *Quinquaginta decisiones*. The new refashioned *Codex (repetitae praelectionis)* was published and came into force in 534 AD. It is divided into twelve books, which in turn are subdivided into *tituli*. The titles contain the constitutions on a specific topic in chronological order.

From the above it should be clear that the most important unit in the whole codification is thus the *titulus*.

The Digest, Institutes and *Codex* formed a unified codification and were the only source of law. New law could only be created by *constitutio*, since the emperor was the only source of law.

Novellae

These are *novellae constitutiones*, new imperial legislation. No official collection of these new constitutions was made, but several private collections were published.

Epitome Juliani. A Latin version of 124 constitutions from 535-555 AD composed by *Julianus*, Julian, a professor of law in Constantinople.

Authenticum. A Latin collection of 134 *novellae* from 535-556 AD which was in later times thought to be the original text.

Collectio Graeca. The Greek collection which contained the original text, consisted of 168 Novels.

Justinian's codification lacked a name and the description *Corpus Iuris Civilis* was introduced by Gothofredus in 1583.

ROMAN LAW AFTER JUSTINIAN

In the eastern Greek-speaking empire, the unfamiliar Latin language made use of the codification difficult, with the result that translations, synopses, simplified and abbreviated versions appeared. The development towards simplification characterized the post-Justinianic law and legal science. However, even in simplified form Justinian's law heavily influenced the eastern-European legal systems.

After the reconquest of Italy the Justinianic codification was introduced in 554 AD, but was soon ousted by the Germanic systems.

At the end of the eleventh century the Digest was rediscovered and Italy saw a strong revival of the study of Roman law.

CHAPTER II – The law of procedure

1. General

Roman law developed from the law of procedure. *Ubi remedium, ibi ius*, where you have a legal remedy you have a right, which implies that the grant of new actions by the *praetor* created new law. The Roman jurist was only interested in the question, whether there was a legal remedy available to his client. From the decisions given in individual cases general rules and principles were distilled at a later stage.

The law of procedure became applicable when somebody claimed that his right had been, or was infringed upon and he wishes to remedy this situation. At a very early stage self-help was the only solution, but the advantages of this method are obvious; might is right, which means that the stronger person is always successful. Therefore, the state intervened by regulating self-help. Self-help became permissible only after the state had satisfied itself that there was indeed a dispute and after the parties had followed a prescribed process to decide which of the parties was correct. Eventually self-help was completely eliminated and the state took charge of the whole process of legal redress.

The functions of the law of procedure are twofold. In the first place the obtaining of a decision in a legal dispute, but secondly the enforcement of the judgment in cases where the defendant lost his case, but did not voluntarily satisfy the plaintiff.

STEPS THAT HAVE TO BE TAKEN IN A LEGAL DISPUTE

Firstly, both parties, the *actor*, plaintiff and the *reus*, defendant, had to appear before the correct instance. Both parties had to be free Roman citizens above the age of puberty.

Secondly, the dispute had to be formulated. Originally this took place by pronouncing prescribed formal words and performing prescribed formal acts, but at a later stage by way of document(s).

Thirdly evidence was submitted and each party pleaded his case. There were few rules regarding evidence and the parties made use of the services of *oratores*, orators, to plead their case.

Finally, a judgment was given. This judgment, called *sententia*, could be in favour of the defendant, acquittal, or in favour of the plaintiff, in which case the condemnation was always for money.

2. Division into two stages of the Roman process

Roman legal procedure was divided into two separate stages, the assertion of claims before the magistrate *in iure* and the actual hearing and decision of the case *apud iudicem*.

IN IURE

The first stage of the process took place before the instance in charge of *iurisdictio*. Originally this was a pontiff thereafter, the *consul* and from 367 BC the *praetor* and from 242 BC the *praetor urbanus* and the *praetor peregrinus* in Rome. On *dies fasti*, days on which litigation was allowed, the *praetor* had his seat on the *forum*, the market-place, and gave assistance to the parties. He explained the law and thus gave information; he granted or refused an action, assisted in formulating the dispute and finally, referred the case to a judge.

The *praetor* did not himself pronounce the final judgment, but merely had an introductory function.

APUD IUDICEM

This was the second stage when the proceedings were carried on *apud iudicem*, before a judge. The judge was a private person which the parties chose from the *album iudicum selectorum*, a list of judges.

Both *praetor* and judge were usually not jurists and would, if necessary, consult jurists.

3. Some basic notions

IN IUS VOCATIO

The first step in any proceeding was the *in ius vocatio*, the summons to appear *in iure*. The initiative was with the plaintiff, who by pronouncing formal words summoned the defendant. If the latter refused to appear, the plaintiff could forcibly take him.

If the defendant could not or did not want to appear immediately, he could provide a *vindex* to act as surety that he would appear. If the defendant did not appear nor provided a *vindex*, the *praetor* could authorize the plaintiff to take over the property of the defendant, *missio in possessionem*.

LITIS CONTESTATIO

Litis contestatio, the joinder of issue, was reached when the proceedings *in iure* were terminated. The dispute was formulated and the parties were no longer allowed to change anything in it.

The most important effect of *litis contestatio* was *ne bis in idem*, the same suit cannot be instituted a second time.

This meant that the *litis contestatio* destroyed or consumed the action; an action could not be brought again in respect of the same matter.

EXECUTION

If a judgment had not been honoured, execution was the procedure that had to be followed to enforce the judgment.

4. Various systems of litigation

LEGISACTIO-PROCEDURE

Originally the Romans used the *legisactio*-procedure, which was characterized by formalism of acts and oral declaration. These formalities dated back to religious rituals, but were later embodied in laws. The prescribed formularies only made provision for a limited number of *casus*, cases, and the strict formalism did not create the possibility of bringing the growing number of new disputes within the sphere of the law. These new disputes arose, as Roman society developed from a small agricultural community, into an expanding state, where trade and industry took over from agriculture.

PROCEDURE PER FORMULAM

Consequently, there came into existence a new system of procedure. This new procedure was used first before the *praetor peregrinus*, who made use of *ius gentium* and was therefore, not bound by the strict formalism of the *ius civile*. In the new system the parties' dispute was formulated in a document, the so-called *formula* and this method of litigation is known as the procedure *per formulam*.

The *lex Aebutia* decreed in about 200 BC, that Roman citizens could litigate in this manner and two *leges Juliae* of Augustus abolished the *legisactio*-procedure in 17 BC. The available *formulae* were published by the *praetor* in his edict, but whenever a new case arose for which there was no appropriate *formula* in the edict, which meant that the aggrieved party had no remedy and the case fell outside the scope of the law, the *praetor* could, by way of his *ius edicendi* introduce a new *formula* in the edict, which, in effect created a new action and extended the law.

COGNITO-PROCEDURE

During the empire the emperor and his bureaucracy, gradually asserted themselves in the field of the administration of justice and introduced a new type of procedure. As the importance of the *praetor* waned the procedure *per formulam* fell into disuse and the new procedure which began as an extraordinary procedure, *cognitio extraordinaria*, became the exclusive mode of procedure during the dominate. The *cognitio*-procedure had little importance as far as the development of Roman law was concerned, but laid the foundations of the modern law of procedure. Where in the preceding systems the actual process played an important role in the development of the substantive law, the *cognitio*-process merely applied the existing law. The most important characteristics of the *cognitio*-procedure were that the state, through appointed officials resolved the differences of her subjects. The whole process took place in front of the same official and there was no longer a division into two stages.

Since there existed a bureaucratic hierarchy of officials, the possibility of appeals, which had not existed in the previous systems, was another important development.

5. Legisactio-procedure

The term *legisactio* has the following meaning. The *actio* was the ritual assertion of claim and denial before a magistrate, thus the procedure which had to be followed by the parties for a process. These procedures, the formal pronouncements and formal acts were embodied in *leges*. The term *actio* had, however, another more common meaning, namely action, the remedy to protect a right like the *actio empti, actio legis Aquiliae, rei vindicatio* etc. There were as many actions as there were rights.

As listed by Gaius, there were five *legisactiones* three of which were procedures to settle a dispute, while the other two were procedures to enforce a judgment.

LEGISACTIO SACRAMENTO

This was the oldest procedure to settle a dispute and could be used both *in rem* and *in personam*, that is, to resolve a dispute concerning a real right or a dispute concerning a personal right.

LEGISACTIO SACRAMENTO IN REM

The first step in any proceeding was the *in ius vocatio*. The plaintiff by use of formal words summoned the defendant to appear with the thing in dispute before the *praetor*.

Laying his hand on the thing, he made a formal claim that the thing was his and touched the thing with a *festuca*, rod. If the defendant defended the claim, he then did exactly the same. The *praetor* then bade both parties to leave the thing alone *'Mittete ambo hominem'*.

After further formal words the parties challenged each other to pledge a *sacramentum*. This was originally a sacrifice to the gods, but became, as the ritualistic aspect of the procedure disappeared, a sum of money which each party pledged as a guarantee of his right. The party in whose favour the judges decision went, got his money back, while the other party's money went to the state. This resulted in unnecessary litigation being kept to a minimum. The *praetor* then awarded interim possession of the thing to one of the parties for the duration of the process. The interim possessor had to provide security in the form of sureties that he would properly look after the thing and restore the thing in case judgment was given against him.

At this stage *litis contestatio*, joinder of issue, ended the procedure *in iure*. The parties had, however, to return *in iure* after 30 days to select a *iudex*, judge.

APUD IUDICEM

The parties lead evidence and plead their case before the judge. At the end of the hearing, the judge gave his decision.

EXECUTION

Should the decision have gone in favour of the party presently in possession, nothing further was necessary. If the judge found for the party not in possession and the one who was in possession refused to restore the thing to him, this party could bring the necessary pressure upon the sureties to enforce the judgment.

LEGIS ACTIO SACRAMENTO IN PERSONAM

The first step was the *in ius vocatio*. When both parties appeared *in iure*, before the *praetor*, the plaintiff made a formal claim that the other party owed him something and gave reasons why. The defendant made an equally formal denial. Then followed the mutual *sacramenta* and *litis contestatio*. After 30 days the *praetor* appointed a judge and the procedure continued *apud iudicem* where it ended with the judge's decision.

EXECUTION

If the decision was in favour of the plaintiff and the defendant refused to comply with the judgment and there were no sureties then execution had to be taken by way of the *legisactio per manus iniectionem*.

The limitations of the *legisactio sacramento* were found in the fact that the formal words in which the dispute had to be framed only made provision for a limited number of *casus*, cases. When Roman society developed and the development of Roman law became a necessity, two new *legisactiones* were introduced to cover new cases of disputes and to simplify the procedure.

LEGISACTIO PER IUDICIS ARBITRIVE POSTULATIONEM

This procedure was already mentioned in the Twelve Tables and could be used only in those cases for which a *lex* prescribed it. As new cases arose which were not covered by the existing procedures, a *lex* was passed to make it possible to settle them by means of this procedure. There was no *sacramentum* in this form of process and the judge was nominated immediately, which made this procedure less expensive and quicker.

LEGISACTIO PER CONDICTIONEM

This *legis actio* was by a *lex Silia* and a *lex Calpurnia* from about 200 BC, to settle disputes concerning a personal right. The claim had to be for a *certa pecunia*, a specific sum of money, or for a *certa res*, a specific thing.

After the *in ius vocatio*, the plaintiff asserted *in iure* by way of formal words that the defendant ought to give him a certain sum of money, or a certain thing, but did not mention the ground for his claim, in other words the source of the alleged debt. This made it possible to extend the law by providing a blanket formulation under which the developing new sources of claims could be enforced. As new circumstances arose which had to be recognized by law as sources of claims, these claims could be settled by means of this procedure, which was introduced to help fill the lacunae, of the old law. Once the dispute had been framed *in iure*, thirty days after *litiscontestatio*, a judge was nominated by the *praetor* and the next step, *apud iudicem*, followed.

If the plaintiff succeeded, it might be necessary to execute the judgment against an unwilling defendant by way of *legisactio per manus iniectionem*.

6. Means of execution in the legisactio-procedure

Execution ensued of an unsuccessful defendant, in a dispute concerning a personal right did not voluntarily satisfy the claim. An unwilling, unsuccessful defendant in a dispute concerning a real right was forced to comply with the judgment by the pressure on his sureties.

LEGISACTIO PER MANUS INIECTIONEM

This was the oldest and most important procedure for execution of a judgment, with primitive undertones in the sense that the execution was aimed at the person of the *iudicatus*, condemned person, of the *confessus*, the defendant, who formally acknowledged the claim *in iure*; cf *confessus pro iudicato habetur*, a *confessus* is in the same position as a condemned person.

After judgment or *confessio*, there was a respite of thirty days, after which the successful plaintiff brought the unsuccessful defendant before the *praetor* by way of *in ius vocation*. *In iure* the plaintiff laid his hands on the defendant and said formally that since the latter was condemned to pay a certain sum of money and since this money had not been paid, he therefore, seized his person. The debtor could not defend himself against this *manus iniectio*, but another person, called a *vindex*, would have to present himself on the defendant's behalf. In a normal situation nobody would be prepared to act as *vindex* and the *praetor* addicted the debtor to the plaintiff. The creditor could take the debtor home, where he could shackle and fetter him. He could keep him for sixty days, during which period he had to produce his prisoner in public on three successive market days and state the amount of the debt, in the hope that someone would settle it to release the debtor. If this did not happen, the creditor could kill the prisoner or sell him as a slave *trans Tiberim*, on the other side of the river Tiber, in a foreign country. If there were several creditors they could cut the debtor to pieces. Around 300 BC the killing and selling as a slave disappeared from practice and the judgment debtor had to work off the amount of his debt.

If the plaintiff had made a mistake and the defendant was not really *iudicatus* or *confessus*, a *vindex* would present himself to defend the defendant. The *vindex* took the defendant's place and the original defendant was released and had nothing to do with the further proceedings. A new process followed between the plaintiff and the *vindex*, on the question whether the original defendant had been *iudicatus* or *confessus* and whether the judgment had been honoured. Assuming a decision in favour of the plaintiff, the *vindex* was condemned to pay twice the original amount.

LEGISACTIO PER PIGNORIS CAPIONEM

This was execution against the property of the defendant. The successful plaintiff seized property of the defendant while uttering certain formal words in front of witnesses. He could retain the property as security, but had no power of sale or otherwise. Moreover, this method was authorized in only a limited number of cases.

7. Formula-procedure

The essence of the formulary process was that the dispute between the parties was formulated in a *formula*, a document in which both the plaintiff's claim and the defendant's defence were framed, in other words wherein the dispute was formulated.

The *praetor* published in his edict examples of available *formulae* of existing actions and whenever the need arose he could by reason of his *ius edicendi* introduce new *formulae* in the edict and thus extend the law.

THE COURSE OF A FORMULA PROCESS

The plaintiff still brought the defendant, by way of the *in ius vocatio*, before the *praetor, in iure.*

IN IURE

Once the parties were before the *praetor*, the plaintiff indicated the nature of his case, *editio actionis*, and asked for the relevant action, *postulatio actionis*. The *praetor* could grant an action, *dare actionem*, or refuse to grant an action, *denegare actionem*. If the *praetor* granted an action, the defendant could either acknowledge the claim, *(confessus pro iudicatio habetur)* or remain passive, *indefensus*, or defend the action. In the last case the parties formulated their dispute under supervision and with the assistance of the *praetor*. Once the *formula* was settled to the satisfaction of the parties and the *praetor, litiscontestatio* was reached, with the result that the *formula* could not be altered and *ne bis in idem*.

APUD IUDICEM

The parties appeared with the *formula* before the judge, a private person selected by themselves. They presented their case themselves or used orators. Evidence was led to prove their assertions, however, there were few rules on evidence. After the final speech by the orators, the judge consulted a *consilium* of jurists and gave his decision, the judgment was always for money. The possibility of appeal did not exist, since the parties had selected the judge themselves and a hierarchy of judges did not exist.

8. Execution

If judgment was given in favour of the plaintiff and the defendant could not or would not comply with the judgment, the plaintiff could after thirty days again take the debtor before the *praetor*.

In iure he would ask for the *actio iudicati*. If the debtor wanted to defend this action, he would have to provide security for twice the original judgment, a *formula* was then drafted and the parties appeared in front of a judge. The judge had to decide whether the defendant was indeed *iudicatus* against the plaintiff and whether he had not honoured the judgment. If the judge found in favour of the plaintiff the defendant would be sentenced to double the amount of the original judgment. In the normal course of things a *iudicatus* would not defend the *actio iudicati* and execution took its course.

The first possibility was that the *praetor* granted a *decretum*, decree, authorizing the plaintiff to seize the debtor physically and he then had to work off his debt.

If, however, the debtor had assets, the second possibility would be preferred, where the *praetor* decreed *missio in possessionem*, seizure of the estate. The assets of the estate were sold, *venditio bonorum*, and the plaintiff and other creditors would be paid from the proceeds.

9. Elements of the formula

The dispute was concisely drafted in the *formula*, setting out the claims and defences of the respective parties. Each *formula* can be divided into several parts, some of which had to appear in each *formula*, while others only appeared in certain circumstances.

CLAUSES FOUND IN EVERY FORMULA

The first part of any *formula* was the *nominatio iudicis*, the nomination of the judge. The parties selected the judge from the *album iudicem selectorum*, but the judge received his appointment and directions from the *praetor*.

The second *sine qua non* of everly *formula* was the *intentio*, the statement of claim.

The form of the *intentio* showed the kind of action in issue. The *intentio* of an *actio in rem* mentioned only the plaintiff's name, since the real right could be enforced against anybody who infringed upon it. The *intentio* of an *actio in personam* mentioned the names of both parties, because the personal right which was enforced, could only be enforced against that particular person.

The *intentio* in such an action revealed whether the perfomance which was claimed was *certum*, specific, or *incertum*, indefinite. The claim was formulated hypothetically, *Si paret* . . ., If it appears . . ., which means that the defence of simple denial was automatically inserted in the *formula*.

The *intentio* was an unfinished sentence and was completed by the following clause, the *condemnatio*.

This clause was a direction to the judge to condemn the defendant to the plaintiff or to absolve him, depending on his finding. The *condemnatio* was always *pecuniaria*, that is the direction to the judge was to condemn for a sum of money.

The *condemnatio* could be *certa*, for a specific sum of money, or *incerta*, in which case the judge had to asses the amount.

It should be stressed, that in the formulary procedure at no stage could the judge order specific performance, for example, return of the thing.

Consequently, there appeared in the *formula* of many actions, the so-called *clausula arbitraria*, which gave the defendant the option of returning the thing in issue and thus to be absolved.

POSSIBLE CLAUSES IN THE FORMULA

In general the *intentio* came immediately after the *nominatio iudicis*, but it could be preceded by another clause, the *demonstratio*. The *intentio*, the claim was based on facts, but did not mention these facts. This was done by the *demonstratio* which was an explanatory clause, setting out the facts from which the claim arose. The *demonstratio* was only found in personal actions claiming an *incertum*.

All personal actions based on the *bona fides*, good faith, claimed an *incertum* and had, therefore, a *demonstratio* in their *formula*.

In the divisory actions the judge had to make an *adiudicatio*, allocating shares of the common property to each of the parties. In the *formulae* of these actions the *adiudicatio* replaces the *condemnatio*.

Another important clause in some *formulae* was the *exceptio*, a special defence against the claim, which was inserted in the *formula* at the request of the defendant. Although some *exceptiones* derived from the *ius civile*, the important *exceptiones* were introduced by the *praetor* to make the strict *ius civile* more equitable; *exceptio doli*, the defense of fraud; the *exceptio metus causa*, the defence of coercion or duress; the *exceptio pacti conventi*, the defence that the plaintiff had informally agreed otherwise.

These *exceptiones* had to be expressly inserted in the *formulae* of *actiones stricti iuris*, but did not need to be made express in the *formulae* of *actiones bonae fidei*, since the matter in issue was to be decided on the basis of good faith.

Further clauses to be mentioned were the *replicatio*, the plaintiff's reply to the *exceptio*; the *duplicatio*, the defendant's riposte to the *replicatio*; and the *triplicatio*, the plaintiff's reply to the *duplicatio*.

Another clause which could be incorporated in the *formula* was the *praescriptio*, a reservation in favour of the plaintiff, *praescriptio pro actore*, or for the defendant, *praescriptio pro reo*. The latter was replaced by the *exceptio*, while the principal function of the former was to prevent consumption through *litiscontestatio* of the present action, of the whole claim against the defendant.

A *praescriptio* was inserted to limit the action to what was now due and reserved rights from the same transaction to prevent *ne bis in idem*.

10. Classification of actions

The fundamental division of actions is into *actiones in rem* and *actiones in personam*.

The *actio in rem* can be instituted against anybody. The *intentio* of the *formula* mentioned only the plaintiff's name, since the real right could be enforced against anybody. In other words, the *actio in rem* enforces the *ius in rem*, the real right, that is binding on all persons; the holder of a real right can institute his action against anybody interfering with his right. Everybody has to respect the real right.

The *actio in personam* only be instituted against a specific person. The name of that person was mentioned together with the plaintiff's name in the *intentio* of the *formula*, since only that person has a duty to perform to the plaintiff.

The *actio in personam* enforces the *ius in personam*, the personal right, that is binding on one particular person. Only this person, the debtor, can infringe on this right. The rest of the world has nothing to do with the relationship between the creditor and the debtor.

Actions could also be distinguished into *actiones bonae fidei* and *actiones stricti iuris*. In the *intentio* of the *actio bonae fidei*, action based on good faith, appeared the words *'ex fide bona'*, which meant that the defendant had to perform according to the requirements of good faith and the judge had, therefore, to decide in accordance with good faith.

The *actio stricti iuris*, action from the strict law, was an action of the old *ius civile*, characterized by its strict formalism, which gave the judge no discretion.

The *praetor* introduced the *exceptiones* to eliminate inequities which could result from this strict formalism.

Furthermore, actions might be *civilis* or *honoraria*. An *actio civilis* was an action from the *ius civile*. With the assistance of the jurists the *praetor* drafted a *formula*, which reflected the verbal declarations of the *legisactio*, called a *formula in ius concepta*.

An actio *honoraria* was an action which was created by the *praetor* or another magistrate with *ius edicendi*. In cases where the *ius civile* did not provide an action, the *praetor*, because he looked after the administration of justice and consequently had *ius edicendi*, could create a new action. With the assistance of the jurists he drafted a new *formula* for the case in question, *formula in factum concepta* and incorporated this in his edict.

11. Different kinds of actiones honorariae

Honorary actions could be one of three types, *in factum*, *ficticia* or *utilis*.

In the *actio in factum*, the action based on fact, the *praetor* took a factual situation as the basis of the *formula* and directed the judge to condemn, if he found the facts established.

The *actio ficticia*, the action based on a fiction, was an adaptation of a civil action to cases to which the civil action was not applicable. In the *formula* of the *actio ficticia* the judge was directed to assume the existence of facts which would make the civil action appropriate to the case in question.

Finally, the praetor introduced the *actio utilis*, analogous action, which extended an existing action.

12. Extraordinary remedies

The abovementioned actions were all part of the *ius honorarium*, but the *ius honorarium* consisted of more than just actions. The *praetor* granted other types of remedies, viz, the *exceptiones, missio in possessionem, restitutio in integrum* and *interdicta*.

RESTITUTIO IN INTEGRUM

The *praetor* promised in his edict, that in certain circumstances, he would nullify a transaction. Although the transaction in question was perfectly valid at civil law, if the consequences turned out to be unfair in the particular instance then restoration of the *status ante quo* was granted by decree, after enquiry by the *praetor*.

INTERDICTA

An *interdictum*, interdict, was a praetorian order. In the edict, the *praetor* promised that in certain circumstances he would grant an order. This order could be positive or negative, i.e. an order to do something or not to do something.

Interdicts could be distinguished as *interdicta prohibitoria, restitutoria* and *exhibitoria. Interdicta prohibitoria*, prohibitory interdicts, were orders to prevent wrongful interference. *Interdicta restitutoria*, restitutory interdicts, were orders to restore something. *Interdicta exhibitoria*, exhibitory interdicts, were orders to produce something.

Interdicts were introduced to protect a right at short notice or to provide a remedy for a case for which there was no action. Some interdicts were final, but others were only provisional orders. The procedure of enforcement was complicated.

13. Cognitio extraordinaria-procedure

The most important characteristic of the *cognitio* procedure was the dominating role of the state.

THE COURSE OF THE COGNITIO PROCESS

The plaintiff submitted his written statement of claim, *libellus conventionis*, to the appropriate court and requested the court to summon the defendant. A court official served the *libellus conventionis* on the defendant. The defendant was instructed to appear on a certain date and to enter a defence, *libellus contradictionis*, before that date.

Assuming the appearance of both parties, the cases on either side were presented by advocates. The adjudicating magistrate subpoenaed witnesses and ruled on evidence, following imperial legislation which had created a law of evidence. The eventual judgment was written and read in court in the presence of the parties.

The judgment was no longer necessarily for money, but could be for specific performance, depending on the nature of the claim.

An important development was the possibility of appeal since there was a hierarchy of courts with the emperor as a court of final instance.

EXECUTION

If the defendant failed to satisfy the judgment the plaintiff requested, by means of the *actio iudicati*, that the authorities took steps to execute the judgment. If the judgment was for specific performance the defendant could be forced to perform *manu militari*, by armed hand, or the court officers took part of the defendant's property to sell by auction. Execution against the person was still possible, but the debtor was confined to a public prison.

CHAPTER III – The law of things

The Roman law of things covered a wider field than our modern classification. Gaius' and Justinian's Institutes divided private law into *ius quod ad personas* (law of persons), *quod ad res* (literally law of things but equivalent to the modern law of property, succession and obligations) and *quod ad actiones* (the law of actions) *pertinet*. In modern law a different scheme is adopted and the law of things is restricted to the law relating to things and real rights, while the law of succession and the law of obligations are considered separate sections of private law.

1. What is a res

The concept *res* underwent a development in Roman law. Originally, in the primitive law of the unsophisticated community of farmers, only that which a person could see, touch, hold, possess, use and enjoy, in short those things which were concretely of service to him, were of interest. In this context it is clear that the original *res* of Roman law were the physical things, *quae tangi possunt*, which could be touched, which could be possessed and used by the person.

During the late republic, as Rome and the Romans had developed, the notion that there are things that cannot be touched but are deemed to exist, came to the fore. Influenced by philosophy, intangibles like the Gods and abstract creations of the human mind were treated by developed Roman jurisprudence as *res*. Everything that could be part of a person's estate, everything of monetary value or appraisable in money, in short all economic assets, corporeal or not, were eventually considered *res*. The practical implication was that not only physical things, but also real rights as well as personal rights, were regarded as *res*.

2. Various classifications of things

The jurists started to systematize Roman law and the following divisions were recognized. Unless stated otherwise the classifications pertained to *res corporalis*.

RES IN NOSTRO PATRIMONIO & RES EXTRA NOSTRUM PATRIMONIUM

Res in nostro patrimonio, things in our estate, or *res in commercio*, things within the trade, were those things, which were or could be in the ownership of individuals.

Res extra nostrum patrimonium, things outside our estate, or *res extra commercium*, things outside the trade, could not be owned by individuals.

The *res extra commercium* were then sub-classified in *res divini iuris*, things subject to divine law, and *res humani iuris*, things subject to human law.

Those *divini iuris* were *res sacrae, religiosae* and *sanctae;* those *humani iuris* were *res communes, publicae* and *universitatis.*

Res sacrae were things dedicated to the heavenly gods, *religiosae* were things consecrated to the nether gods and *sanctae* were placed under the protection of the gods.

Res communes were things belonging to everyone for common use and enjoyment, for example the air, the sea etc. *Res publicae* belonged to the state for use and enjoyment of its citizens, such as public roads, bridges etc, while *res universitatis* were things which belonged to a city for the use and enjoyment of its inhabitants.

Since the *res in nostio patrimonio* were, for obvious reasons, more important the following divisions applied to these things only.

RES CORPORALES & RES INCORPORALES

Res corporales are physical things, *quae tangi possunt*, which can be touched or which can be perceived by the senses.

Res incorporales are incorporeal things, *quae tangi non possunt*, which cannot be touched. They are abstract conceptions recognized and protected by law, such as real and personal rights.

Ownership, however, was not considered to be a *res incorporalis* by the Roman lawyers and only *res corporales* could be the object of ownership.

Moreover, only corporeal things could be possessed and consequently a number of legal concepts where possession played an essential part were not applicable to *res incorporales.*

RES MANCIPI & RES NEC MANCIPI

In preclassical and classical Roman law this was the most important legal classification of things *in commercio.*

Res mancipi were land and buildings in Italy, beasts of draught and burden, slaves and rustic praedial servitudes.

Since *res mancipi* were the most important assets in the early Roman agricultural society, ownership had to be transferred in a formal manner by way of *mancipatio* or *in iure cessio.* When *res mancipi* were transferred informally by *traditio* only possession but not ownership was transferred and this led to the emergence of bonitary or praetorian ownership.

Mancipatio and *in iure cessio* fell into desuetude in late classical law and Justinian expressly abolished both the formal methods of transferring ownership as well as the distinction between *res mancipi* and *res nec mancipi*.

Res nec mancipi were all things which were not *res mancipi*.

Ownership could be transferred informally by way of *traditio* or in a formal manner by *in iure cessio*.

RES MOBILES & RES IMMOBILES

Res immobiles, immovable things, were land and everything permanently annexed to it.

Res mobiles, movable things, were all things which were not immovables.

In Roman law this distinction had less significance than today but it played a role with regard to *usucapio, accessio*, protection of possession and *furtum*.

LAND

During the republic a distinction was made between land in Rome and land in Italy, the so-called *ager publicus*. Land in Rome was privately owned but the ownership of the *ager publicus*, public land, was vested in the Roman people. This land became private property towards the end of the republic when a new distinction was made, namely between land in Italy and provincial land. Italic land was privately owned but the ownership of provincial land vested in the state, in either the *populus* or the emperor.

SPECIES & GENUS RES

Species res is a specific thing.

Genus res is a generic thing, that is a thing that is specified according to type.

Genera non pereunt means that generic performance is never objectively impossible.

RES FUNGIBILES & RES NON FUNGIBILES

Res fungibiles are things that can be replaced and are therefore generic things.

Res non fungibiles, things which cannot be replaced are specific things.

RES CONSUMPTIBILES & RES NON CONSUMPTIBILES

Res consumptibiles are things that are consumed by normal use, while *res non consumptibiles* are not. In general generic things are *consumptibiles*. This difference had legal importance with regard to the different contracts of loan as well as usufruct.

Furthermore, there are divisible things against indivisibles and single things against collective things.

FRUCTUS

Fructus, fruits produced by a thing become separate things by separation. *Fructus* could be *naturales* or *civiles*, the latter arising from the use of the property e.g. the rent of houses or the earnings of slaves. *Fructus naturales* were the ordinary natural produce of a thing, such as the fruits of an orchard or the young of animals.

Fructus naturales could be further divided into *fructus pendentes*, hanging fruits, those not yet separated, *fructus separati*, separated fruits, and *fructus percepti*, fruits separated and gathered. These distinctions are relevant with regard to the acquisition of ownership of fruits.

3. Real rights

Iura in re or *rem*, real rights or the so-called absolute rights, have effect against the whole world. The holder of such a right can institute his action, an *actio in rem*, against anybody who has infringed upon his right. In short the whole world has to respect his right.

The *iura in re* are limited in number and can be classified into *iura in re propria* and *iura in re aliena. Iura in re propria*, rights over your own property, is ownership and *iura in re aliena*, rights over someone else's property. The latter are, as a rule, grouped under three heads, i.e. servitudes, long term leases and real security. Since real rights have effect against the whole world, it follows that a *ius in re aliena* cannot be defeated by transfer of ownership.

4. Ownership

Ownership is the most extensive right that a person can have in a corporeal thing. It is the absolute right to do with his thing whatever pleases him, the *ius utendi, fruendi et abutendi*, the right to use, enjoy and consume, abuse and alienate the thing. In short, the owner can commit nearly any factual or legal act with relation to his property. Roman law knew two types of ownership, namely *dominium ex iure Quiritium* and bonitary or praetorian ownership.

Dominium ex iure Quiritium was ownership according to the *ius civile*. Only Roman citizens or persons with *ius commercii* could have this type of ownership.

Praetorian or bonitary ownership originated as a result of interference by the *praetor*.

If *res mancipi* were transferred informally by *traditio*, the transferee did not get *dominium* but would have the thing *in bonis*, among his possessions. The transferor remained *dominus ex iure Quiritium* and the transferee would have to possess the thing for one or two years to become *dominus* by means of *usucapio*. Originally, the transferee's possession during the period of *usucapio* was not protected but the *praetor* intervened by giving him the *actio publiciana* and the *exceptio rei venditae ac traditae*.

The *actio publiciana* was an *actio ficticia*, with exactly the same effect as the *reivindicatio* of the *dominus;* it was an *actio in rem* by means of which the transferee reclaimed possession during the period of *usucapio* from whoever may have held it without title, irrespective whether such person was *bona fide* or *mala fide*. The *exceptio rei venditae ac traditae* was a special defence that the thing had been sold and delivered to him. If the transferee was sued by the *dominus* with the *reivindicatio* during the period of *usucapio*, this defence was granted. The holder thus obtained complete protection during the period of *usucapio* and had all the practical benefits of ownership and was therefore called praetorian or bonitary owner.

As the distinction between *res mancipi* and *res nec mancipi* became obsolete and was eventually abolished by Justinian, only *dominium ex iure Quiritium* was known in his time.

5. Limitations on ownership

The right of ownership could be limited in various ways, by public law, by the rights of neighbours and by voluntary limitation.

There were various limitations in public law on the power of a *dominus* over his property. The criterion in these instances was the public interest and legislation in the interest of public health and safety was not unknown in Roman law. The *censor* also played a role in this regard.

Secondly, any owner could voluntarily limit his right of ownership by giving actual use and enjoyment to others, for instance by lease or usufruct etc.

Finally, the power of an owner over his land was fettered by his neighbour's rights to enjoy their property.

In principle, the owner of land had absolute power over his land, the space above and everything under it. The logical consequence was that buildings or trees were not allowed to hang over a neighbour's property and an owner could refuse entry to his property. As the Roman population increased and neighbours came closer to each other, limitations developed, since unrestricted use, abuse and enjoyment could cause unreasonable inconvenience to neighbours.

Already, the Twelve Tables ruled that overhanging branches could be cut down to a height of fifteen feet and the *interdictum de arboribus caedendis* lay in this respect.

If fruit fell from trees on the adjoining land, the owner was allowed to collect his fruit every second day and his remedy was the *interdictum de glande legenda*. The *actio aquae pluviae ariendae* was aimed at a neighbour who artificially directed the flow of water onto your property.

If a dilapidated structure on the adjoining land threatened the collapse and subsequently to damage your property, the *praetor* could be approached with an application that the owner of the defective premises gave security against possible damage by way of the *cautio damni infecti.* Should he refuse, the *praetor* granted *missio in possessionem*, placing the applicant in the possession of the ruin.

Where the owner of a property built or excavated in such a manner that his neighbour feared possible damage to his own land and buildings, *operis novi nuntiatio* served notice that he had either to cease the work or to give security against possible damage by way of the *cautio damni infecti.* Should he refuse, the *praetor* granted the *interdictum demolitorium* for its demolition.

An owner of land which had no outlet to a public road could claim a way of necessity.

Smoke or the natural flow of water from a neighbour's land had to be accepted within reasonable limits but if it became a nuisance, the *interdictum uti possidetis* could be sought.

A wall could hang half a foot over the neighbour's property.

In case of a dispute with regard to the boundary between the properties, the *actio finium regundorum* applied.

6. Co-ownership

Co-ownership or joint ownership is the ownership which two or more persons have simultaneously in the same thing. Each has the same rights to the thing and in practice severe problems can arise.

VARIOUS FORMS OF CO-OWNERSHIP

The oldest form of joint ownership in Roman law was the *consortium ercto non cito*, which arose from succession. The *sui heredes*, the first group of heirs according to the Twelve Tables, became joint owners of the assets of the deceased estate. A division could, however, be effected by bringing the *actio familiae erciscundae.*

The *communio pro indiviso* or *condominium* was voluntarily entered into as a rule by partners engaged in a business venture. Each joint owner had an individed share in the thing and could use, enjoy and alienate his share of the thing. With regard to the thing as a whole all the joint owners together had power of disposition. Each co-owner had a *ius prohibendi*, the power of veto, whereby he could prohibit other co-owners from abusing the property and the *actio communi dividundo* was the action for division and settling of claims.

7. Acquisition of ownership

Ownership is a real right and has to be acquired in a certain manner. Roman law knew several modes of acquisition of ownership which all depended on the essential characteristic of ownership, namely that it is a right, binding on all persons and consequently the methods required publicity.

The modes of acquisition can be classified into original or derivative methods. Original modes of acquisition of ownership are those where a person acquires the right of ownership over a thing without co-operation and independent of another person. This means that there was no previous owner, the thing in question did not have an owner but could be owned, or there was a previous owner but the latter did not co-operate in the acquisition of ownership.

The derivative methods are those where the owner of a thing transfers the ownership of it to another person. The ownership is passed from one person to another with the co-operation of the first person. In this context, the *nemo plus iuris*-rule applied.

Nemo plus iuris ad alium transferre potest, quam ipse haberet, no one can transfer more rights to another, than he himself had. The practical implication of this rule was, that in principle only the owner could transfer ownership. Thus, in Roman law it was, in principle, impossible to acquire ownership from a *non-dominus*, a non-owner.

A second distinction existed between modes of acquisition deriving from the *ius civile* and those from the *ius gentium*.

The modes *iuris civilis* were those which were typically Roman and strictly formal, *mancipatio, in iure cessio* and *usucapio.*

The modes *iuris gentium* were modes which were used by other peoples as well and were informal, *traditio, occupatio, accessio* etc.

8. Derivative modes of acquisition

The derivative methods of acquisition of ownership are those where the owner of a thing transfers the ownership of it to another person.

The first question that comes forward is, *why does he do this?* The answer is, *because the two parties had agreed to do so.*

There is a reason, a *iusta causa*, for the transfer of ownership, for example a contract of sale.

A second point of interest is stated by the so-called *Regula Diocletiana : traditionibus et usucapionibus dominia rerum, non nudis pactis transferuntur*, ownership is transferred by delivery and prescription, not by agreement only. This means that for the transfer of ownership a separate legal act was required. The contract of sale did not transfer ownership, but was the reason for the actual legal act whereby ownership is transferred. Roman law knew three such transactions, *mancipatio, in iure cessio* and *traditio*.

Both parties had to be Roman citizens or have the *ius commercii*, the right to participate in Roman law.

Finally, the *nemo plus iuris*-rule applied, so the transferor had to be owner.

MANCIPATIO

Mancipatio was an ancient institution already in existence before the Twelve Tables and thus part of the *ius civile* and formal.

In origin *mancipatio* was a combination of a formal cash sale and a mode of transferring *dominium*. Copper was weighed out on the scales, *libra*, as a price and was handed over simultaneously with the transfer of the object sold and a formal declaration was made in front of five witnesses, thus providing publicity.

In the fourth century BC, when coined money appeared, the symbolism of the scales was retained and the scales were touched with a copper coin. Next the *mancipatio* was used to transfer ownership in consequence of a sale on credit or any other reason and thus became a formal mode of transfer of *dominium*.

Moreover, *mancipatio* was adapted to other purposes like the constituting of servitudes, emancipation, adoption, the creation of marital power over a wife, and the making of a will at an early stage.

MANCIPATIO AS MODE OF TRANSFERRING DOMINIUM

Only the ownership of *res mancipi* could be transferred by way of *mancipatio*. Both parties and the thing to be transferred appeared in front of five witnesses and the *libripens,* a person holding scales. Everyone had to be Roman citizens having reached puberty. Taking hold of the thing the transferee declared formally that the thing was his and bought with this copper with which he then touched the scales, before handing it over to the transferor. Assuming that the transferor was owner of the thing, *dominium* passed. Gaius called *mancipatio* a *venditio imaginaria*, a fictitious sale. It is obvious that *mancipatio* as a derivative mode of acquisition took place in consequence of a reason. Invalidity of this reason did not affect the transfer of ownership, i.e. *mancipatio* was abstract.

LIABILITY IN CASE OF EVICTION

If the transferee was evicted, that is if a third person claimed the property with the *reivindicatio* and the challenge was succesful, the transferee had the *actio auctoritatis* against the transferor for double the price. In other words, when the transferor was not the owner of the thing, *dominium* did not pass, even if the *mancipatio* was correctly performed, as a result of the *nemo plus iuris*-rule. If the owner claimed his property, the evicted transferee had the *actio auctoritatis* on the basis of *mancipatio*. Another action which lay in cases of *mancipatio* was the *actio de modo agri*, where the transferred land turned out to be smaller than stated.

Mancipatio become obsolete in post-classical law and was abolished by Justinian.

IN IURE CESSIO

In iure cessio, cession before the *praetor*, was also in existence in the time of the Twelve Tables, part of the *ius civile* and formal.

The ownership of *res mancipi* as well as *res nec mancipi* could be transferred by this method.

Both parties and the thing to be transferred appeared before the *praetor*. The transferee held the thing and formally claimed the object to be his. The transferor remained silent and the *praetor* awarded the thing to the transferee. As a result of the fictitious process ownership was passed with the required publicity. Since *in iure cessio* was formal, it was abstract like *mancipatio*, but in case of eviction no action derived from the *in iure cessio*.

In iure cessio was seldom used to transfer ownership but it could be used in respect of *res incorporales*, for example to create servitudes. It became obsolete in postclassical time and Justinian abolished it.

9. Traditio

The third and final derivative mode of acquisition of ownership was *traditio*, delivery. It originated in the *ius gentium* and was thus informal.

Originally, it could only be used to transfer the ownership of *res nec mancipi* but in late- and post-classical law the ownership of all *res corporales* could be transferred by this method.

Traditio, delivery, is in essence the transfer of possession, i.e. the physical control of a corporeal thing.

It is clear, however, that not every *traditio*, transfer of possession, transfers ownership. We thus come to the question why the transferor delivers the possession to the transferee? He does this in consequence of one or another reason, *causa*, for example he loans the object to the transferee, he donates the thing to him, he deposits the thing with him, he has sold the thing to him or he lets the thing to him etc.

Every delivery takes place in consequence of a *causa* but it is clear that ownership does not pass in every case. Only where there is a *iusta causa*, a good cause, i.e. a transaction in consequence of which ownership usually passes, does delivery transfer ownership.

Iusta causa is not in itself a mode of acquisition but is a basis for acquisition of ownership. A contract of sale for instance did not transfer ownership but is the *causa* in consequence of which ownership is transferred by delivery or *mancipatio* or *in iure cessio* in Roman law. Where there is a *iusta causa*, it is the intention of the parties that ownership is passed. Thus, it is the intention with which the physical transfer is made and received which determines the effect of such transfer and such intention is revealed by the *causa*.

The question whether *traditio* was a causal or an abstract mode of transfer of ownership was not clearly answered by Roman law. In other words the texts are not unanimous in requiring in real, genuinely existing *iusta causa* before the ownership could be passed by delivery but in many instances a putative *causa* would suffice. That means, that if the parties, for example, thought that they had concluded a sale, when in fact they had not, and delivery was made accordingly, ownership passed.

THE CONTRACT OF SALE AS IUSTA CAUSA

The contract of sale is inevitably the most common and important *iusta causa*.

Since Gaius does not mention any special rules in relation to the contract of sale as the *iusta causa traditionis*, ownership is transferred by *traditio* in consequence of a contract of sale.

Justinian stated, however, that when the contract of sale was the *iusta causa traditionis* and subsequent delivery took place, the ownership only passed if the purchase price had been paid or there had been an agreement for credit or security for payment was provided. In other words unless one of these three requirements was met, ownership of the object sold did not pass upon delivery.

The essence of *traditio* is the transfer of possession. Possession is factual, namely the physical control of a corporeal thing and originally physical contact was required. *Traditio* takes place when the transferor hands over the thing to the transferee but complications arise when the thing to be delivered is very big or heavy or immovable. Gradually the concept of possession underwent a change; it became unnecessary to physically hold the thing but was sufficient to be in control of the thing according to the views of the community. Therefore, several new methods of delivery developed, the so-called *traditiones fictae*, fictitious delivery, alongside the *traditio corporalis* or *vera*, actual, real or physical delivery, where the transferor hands over the thing to the transferee, *traditio de manu in manum*, delivery from hand to hand.

TRADITIONES FICTAE

Traditio longa manu, delivery by the long hand, occurred where the transferor points out the thing to the transferee in his presence, so that the latter can exercise control over it.

Traditio brevi manu, delivery by the short hand, occurred where the intended transferee already has physical control of the thing, for example holding it as a lessee and he subsequently buys it. The *nuda voluntas*, bare intent, of the parties transfers the ownership.

Constitutum possessorium is the converse of *traditio brevi manu*. The transferor remains in physical control of the thing, for example he sells the thing but leases it from the buyer. The *nuda voluntas*, bare intent, of the parties transfers the ownership.

Finally, *traditio simbolica*, symbolical delivery, where a symbol of the thing is delivered. In post-classical law documents became generally adopted in legal practice to facilitate proof. It became the practice to record a contract of sale in writing and delivery of the document sufficed to transfer ownership in the later empire.

It should be clear that in later Roman law ownership could be transferred by bare intent of the parties but the normal form of delivery remained the actual handing over of the article by the transferor to the transferee.

10. Original modes of acquisition

Original modes of acquisition of ownership occur when a person acquires the right of ownership of a thing without co-operation and independent of another person. There was no previous owner or, if there was one, he did not co-operate in the acquisition of ownership.

Prescription, occupation, acquisition of fruits, accession and *specificatio* were the original modes of acquisition in Roman law.

PRESCRIPTION

The word 'prescription' is used in two senses, i.e. acquisitive prescription, the Roman *usucapio*, which is the acquisition of ownership in property belonging to another and extinctive prescription, the Roman *longi temporis praescriptio*, which extinguished actions after certain prescribed periods.

USUCAPIO

Usucapio the most important original mode of acquisition was already in existence at the time of the Twelve Tables and thus part of the *ius civile*.

The essence of *usucapio* was that possession of an object which belonged to another after a certain period made the possessor the owner of the thing. The ownership of the previous owner ceased to exist and the new owner acquired a new ownership.

Although *usucapio* could lead to harsh consequences, the legal system needed such an institution for various reasons.

Firstly, *usucapio* provided the necessary certainty with regard to ownership by removing doubt in this regard after the appropriate period. *Usucapio* also played an important role in the law of evidence, since the plaintiff who claimed to be the owner of the thing only had to prove that he had been in possession for the prescribed period instead of having to prove the ownership of his predecessor, for which he also had to prove the ownership of his predecessor's predecessor etc.

Usucapio was the necessary complement to the *nemo plus iuris*-rule. According to this rule the interest of the owner who had lost possession prevailed over the interest of the *bona fide possessor*, but *usucapio* made the *bona fide* possessor who had acquired possession from a non-owner in consequence of a *iusta causa*, the new owner of the thing. Moreover, in pre-classical and classical Roman law *usucapio* transformed bonitary ownership into *dominium*.

REQUIREMENTS OF USUCAPIO

Res habilis

Firstly, the *res* had to be *habilis*, capable of *usucapio*. This generally meant that the thing had to be *in commercio* as well as *res corporalis*, because only those things were possible as objects of private ownership.

Apart from this general principle the thing could be declared ineligible for *usucapio* by a rule of law. The two most important instances of such *res inhabiles* were stolen things according to the Twelve Tables and property taken by force according to the *Lex Julia et Plautia*.

These things, and some other less important *res inhabiles*, suffered from a *vitium*, taint, which prohibited *usucapio*. Only if the *vitium* was expunged, because the object had returned to its owner, did the thing become *res habilis*.

POSSESSIO

The next requirement was possession, i.e. physical control.

The possession had to be uninterrupted for the appropriate period. *Usurpatio* or *interruptio* ended *usucapio* and if possession was subsequently regained the required period of possession started all over again.

Originally, interruption occurred only if possession was lost but in later law the institution of a legal claim was also an *usurpatio*.

An important instance of *interruptio* was where a person in the course of *usucapio* transferred the thing to another. The *usucapio* would have to start all over again.

In classical law the only exception to this rule was that an heir could complete the *usucapio* of the deceased.

Justinian allowed a general addition of periods of possession, the so-called *accessio possessionum* or *temporum*.

IUSTA CAUSA

Iusta causa or *iustus titulus*, a good cause of title, was a transaction in consequence of which ownership in normal circumstances passes.

In normal circumstances *usucapio* did not apply, since the transferee would have become owner by *mancipatio, in iure cessio* or *traditio*, but when the circumstances were not normal, in other words when the transferee did not become owner as the result of the *nemo plus iuris*-rule, *usucapio* applied.

The *iusta causa* had to be real, but exceptions were apparently allowed.

BONA FIDES

Bona fides, good faith, meant that the person who acquired possession of the thing, had to believe that he had acquired ownership.

Mala fides superveniens non nocet, supervening bad faith does not harm. This maxim expresses the principle that the usucaper had to be *bona fide* only at the moment of taking possession and commencing *usucapio;* if he learned the truth later, during the *usucapio*-period, it did not affect his *usucapio.*

When *accessio possessionum* was allowed by Justinian, only the first possessor had to be *bona fide* on acquiring possession.

Bona fides praesumitur, good faith was presumed. There was a rebuttable presumption that the possessor was *bona fide.*

TEMPUS

The period of possession required was short. The Twelve Tables stated two years for land and one year for other things. Justinian extended the period for movables to three years and for immovables to ten years *inter praesentes*, where the original owner resided in the same province, and twenty years *inter absentes*, where the parties were domiciled in different provinces.

LONGI TEMPORIS PRAESCRIPTIO

Being an institution of the *ius civile, usucapio* could be utilized only by Roman citizens or *peregrini* who had the *ius commercii.* Moreover, it was applicable only to *res in commercio.*

Thus there developed in the second century AD a second type of prescription which applied to provincial land and movables in possession of foreigners, namely the *praescriptio longi temporis*, the prescription of long time.

Initially this was only a defence which protected the possessor of provincial land in certain instances against the claim of the person originally entitled to the land. This defence was soon extended to peregrine-possessors of movables and became generally applicable after 212 AD.

REQUIREMENTS FOR PRAESCRIPTIO

Firstly, a *iustum initium possessionis*, a just beginning of possession, was required. This meant, in fact, that a *iusta causa* and *bona fides* were necessary for a successful defence.

Secondly, uninterrupted possession for the appropriate period was required, but *accessio temporum* was always permitted.

Finally, the length of the required period was ten years *inter praesentes* for movables and immovables and twenty years *inter absentes* for movables and immovables.

This form of prescription did not give the possessor ownership, but gave him a defence against the *reivindicatio* of the owner or the special action of the person entitled to the provincial land. This was extinctive prescription.

In Justinian's time all inhabitants of the empire were Roman citizens and provincial land could be privately owned. Thus, Justinian fused *longi temporis praescriptio* and *usucapio*.

LONGISSIMI TEMPORIS PRAESCRIPTIO

At the beginning of the fourth century AD this form of prescription appeared.

A person who had been in possession for a very long time could bar the *reivindicatio* of the owner with this defence. The required period was originally forty years, but was later reduced to thirty years. Justinian made this form of prescription acquisitive by enacting that if the possession was *bona fide* the possessor acquired ownership after thirty years.

11. Occupatio

The taking possession of a *res nullius* with the intention of becoming owner, makes the occupier owner by way of *occupatio*.

Res nullius are things which are capable of ownership, but which are unowned.

EXAMPLES OF RES NULLIUS

Firstly, wild animals, birds, bees and fish came under ownership when they are brought under effective control i.e. captured or killed. As soon as the animal escapes, the ownership is lost and the animal is a *res nullius* again. It makes no difference on whose property the animal is captured. Wounding an animal is not sufficient, since it has to be brought effectively under control.

Partially tame animals like doves and bees continued to be owned as long as they had the *animus revertendi*, the habit of returning.

Occupatio is only applicable to wild animals and never to domestic animals. If the latter escapes and the owner losses possession, he retains ownership and anybody taking possession with the intention of becoming owner, commits theft.

The second example of *res nullius* was war booty, even if this belonged to someone else. Immovables went to the state and movables became the property of whoever took it.

Other examples were things found on the seashore, an *insula in mari nata*, an island arising in the sea, *res derelictae* and *thesaurus*.

Res derelictae, abandoned things are things which the owner thrown away or discarded with the intention of relinguishing his ownership. They would be distinguished from *res deperditae*, lost things, where the owner has the requisite intention of remaining owner even though he has lost physical control of the thing.

Thesaurus, treasure trove, is something valuable, generally buried in land unknown to anybody. Hadrian legislated that a person who found a treasure on his own property, became the owner of it; if he found it on another's property, he became owner of half and the landowner acquired the other half.

12. Acquisition of fruits

When fruits are separated from the thing which produced them and they thus become separate things, the question of the ownership over them becomes topical.

The general rule is that the owner of the thing which produces fruits becomes the owner of the separated fruits.

In some cases, however, fruits are acquired by another person who has a special relation to the main object: the first of these is the usufructuary who becomes owner of the fruits by *perceptio*, gathering. The lessee also has to actually take possession, *perceptio*, to acquire ownership of the fruits.

The *emphyteuticarius* and the *bona fide possessor* acquire ownership of fruits by *separatio*, separation.

13. Accessio

Accessio, accession, was an original method of acquiring ownership in a thing by virtue of it being joined to or incorporated with something already belonging to the acquirer.

This would occur where two separate things belonging to two separate owners, became inseparably joined in that the one was incorporated into the other. It is irrelevant as regards the question of ownership, whether there was a contract between the two parties involved, or whether theft had been committed.

Two questions arise, namely who becomes the owner of the total object and how is the ex-owner of the vanished object compensated?

The basic rule is that the owner of the dominant object becomes the owner of the final thing.

It is, however, difficult to decide what object is the dominant object. This is not necessarily the most valuable object of the two. The criterion used is that the thing which absorbs the other is the dominant object and the absorbed thing is the minor object. This philosophical approach can lead to confusion which combined with the fact that there are numerous exceptions to the rule complicates matters. Moreover, Roman law did not treat *accessio* as a general principle, but approached each case on its own merits. This same casuistry is found with regard to the compensation of the exowner of the minor object. In this context it should be mentioned, that the parties could have contracted in this regard and that in case of theft the applicable actions would be available.

THREE CATEGORIES OF ACCESSIO

Accessio of immovables to immovables

Firstly, the *accessio* of immovables to immovables where four forms all involving riparian owners could be distinguished.

Alluvio

Alluvio, accretion of land, takes place when the flow of a river gradually and imperceptibly adds to the land of a riparian owner. These additions became the property of the relevant owner and although the soil thus accrued was gradually and imperceptibly lost by another riparian owner, no question of redress or compensation arose.

Avulsio

Avulsio, occurred when a sizeable piece of land was torn away by the torrent of the river and thrown against another's land. When trees, plants or grass took root in the adjoining ground the riparian owner acquired the ownership of the detached part by way of *accessio*.

Insula nata in flumine

Insula nata in flumine, an island which arose in a river became the property of the riparian owners, *pro rata*.

Alveus derelictus

Alveus derelictus, a dry riverbed became the property of the riparian owners, *pro rata*. In none of these cases of *accessio* did the question of compensation arise.

Accessio of movables to movables

In these cases it is very difficult or impossible to distinguish between the major and the minor object. Consequently, the solutions of the Roman casuistry are rather varied.

Confusio

Confusio occurred when liquids belonging to two owners were mixed together. The relevant criterion in this instance was whether the mixture was separable or not. In the first case the result was that the two parties owned the mixture in common and each could claim division by way of the *actio communi dividundo*. If separable, for example molten metals, each owner retained ownership in respect of his portion of the mixture. Each owner could effect a separation by instituting the *actio ad exhibendum* and then claim his property by way of the *reivindicatio*.

Commixtio

Commixtio occurred when solids of two owners were mixed together. The relevant criterion was whether this was done by agreement or not. If yes, the result was again common ownership; if no, each owner retained ownership in respect of his portion of the mixture and had an *actio in rem* to recover his appropriate portion.

It should be clear that both *confusio* and *commixtio* were not typical examples of accession.
A better instance of *accessio* was found in *textura*.

Textura

Textura occurred if one person's wool, gold thread etc was woven into another's material. The material was the dominant thing and thus the owner of the material became owner of the thread.

The ex-owner had various remedies depending on the circumstances of the case. If he was in possession of the final product, he could raise the *exceptio doli* against the *reivindicatio* of the owner as long as the latter had not repaid him for his loss. In short he could exercise a lien by way of the *exceptio doli*. If, however, the owner of the final thing was in possession, the ex-owner could, if separation was feasible, institute the *actio ad exhibendum* and, after separation, the *reivindicatio* to reclaim his property. In most cases of *accessio*, however, separation was not feasible and the *praetor* would grant an *actio in factum* or *actio utilis* for the value of the thing incorporated.

It should be mentioned that the availability of various remedies was dependent on being in possession or not of the thing in question.

Ferruminatio

Ferruminatio, welding, in which case the objects were inseparable. The owner of the principal thing became owner of the minor object and the latter had the same remedies available to him as applicable in the case of *textura.*

Plumbatura

Plumbatura, soldering, was, however, separable, so each owner retained his ownership and the *actio ad exhibendum* lay to effect separation.

Scriptura

Scriptura, where someone wrote on somebody else's parchment or paper. The paper is the principal element and thus the owner of the paper became owner of the whole.

The writer had several remedies of which the most important in practice was the *exceptio doli* which applied in the case where the writer was in possession of the document. He could rebut the *reivindicatio* of the owner by raising the *exceptio doli* until the owner had reimbursed him. He had a lien. If the owner was in possession, the *praetor* gave the writer an *actio in factum* or an *actio utilis* to claim compensation.

Pictura

Pictura, where someone painted a picture on someone else's tablet or canvas, had a different solution. The picture was the principal element and thus the painter became owner of the painting.

The ex-owner of the material was granted an *actio utilis* to claim compensation. However, if he was in possession of the painting he could use the *exceptio doli* as in the case of *scriptura.*

Accessio of movables to immovables

In these cases the immovable is without exception the dominant thing.

Inaedificatio

Inaedificatio, where one person's building materials are used upon another's land.

The general rule in these case was *superficies solo credit*, i.e. a building accedes to the land or in other words the owner of the land becomes the owner of anything built upon his land.

With regard to the compensation of the ex-owner of the building material a distinction is relevant, namely between the case where a person builds on his own land with another's materials and the case where a person builds on another's land with his own materials.

In the first case the Twelve Tables forbade the ex-owner of the materials to institute the *actio ad exhibendum*, but gave him the personal *actio de tigno iuncto* for double the value of the materials.

Justinian allowed the ex-owner of the material an additional *actio ad exhibendum* against the *mala fide* builder, i.e. the builder who was aware of the fact that he was building with another's materials.

Finally, if the ex-owner of the materials was prepared to wait until the building was demolished without using the *actio de tigno iuncto*, he could then claim his materials by means of his *reivindicatio*. Theoretically his ownership was suspended so long as the building was standing and was revived when it happened to be demolished.

In the second case where a person builds on another's land with his own materials, the remedies varied according to the good or bad faith of the builder.

A *bona fide* builder is someone who is unaware of the true facts and is convinced that he is the owner of the land in question or otherwise entitled to build there. If the *bona fide* builder was in possession of the land, which would in practice usually have been the case, he could rebut the *reivindicatio* of the owner by raising the *exceptio doli* until he was reimbursed to the value of his materials and labour costs. In short he had a lien.

If the *bona fide* builder did not follow this course, he had a *ius tollendi*, a right to remove his materials, if he could do so without harm to the site, or he could wait until the building was demolished one day and then claim his materials by way of the *reivindicatio*.

The *mala fide* builder, i.e. the builder who was aware of the fact that he was building on another's property and that he was not entitled to do so, had in principle no claim for compensation. The point of view was that he had donated his materials to the owner of the land. However, there are texts that grant a *ius tollendi* to the *mala fide* builder as well or even an action to claim compensation from the owner.

IMPLANTATIO AND SATIO

Implantatio occurred when one person planted a tree or plant in the land of another, while *satio* was where seeds of one person were sown in the land of another. As soon as plant, tree or seed started growing, it became the property of the landowner.

The original owner of plant, tree or seed could, if he was in possession of the land, rebut the *reivindicatio* of the landowner with an *exceptio doli* until he was reimbursed. Otherwise the *praetor* would grant him an *actio utilis* to claim compensation.

14. Specificatio

Specificatio occurred where one person created a new thing out of materials belonging to another.

The Sabinians were of the opinion that the owner of the materials acquired the ownership of the new thing, while the Proculians held the view that the maker acquired ownership of the thing he had created. Justinian adopted a middle view and ruled that if the new thing could be reduced to its former materials, the owner of the material became owner of the new thing. If this could not be done, the maker became the owner.

When someone created a new thing out of his own material and out of another's material the case was classified as *specificatio*, but was really *accessio*, since in this case the maker always became the owner of the new thing.

The party who suffered loss had a claim against the owner by way of an *actio utilis*.

15. Protection of ownership

There were various remedies available to the owner depending on the way in which his ownership was infringed. For example, in the case of theft, the owner could recover his property by means of the *reivindicatio*, he could institute the *actio furti* to punish the thief and if recovery of the stolen property was impossible the *condictio furtiva* lay for damages. The owner of immovable property had the various actions and interdicts available in cases of nuisance, the *actio negatoria* and in general any owner could apply the possessory interdicts.

The most important remedy, however, was the *reivindicatio*, by which action he recovered lost possession of his thing. In practice another action was employed before the owner made use of his *reivindicatio* namely the *actio ad exhibendum*.

16. Actio ad exhibendum

Since the *reivindicatio* had to be instituted against the possessor, it was necessary to determine in whose possession the thing was. In addition, not only the parties, but also the thing in dispute had to appear before the *praetor*.

Thus, the *actio ad exhibendum* was in fact a prerequisite for the *reivindicatio*. The *actio ad exhibendum* was an *actio in personam* from the *ius civile* used to determine whether a certain person was in possession of a thing and if this was the case to force that person to produce the thing.

This action lay not only for the owner of the thing, but for any person who wanted the object to be produced. Thus, this action played an important role in *accessio*. The plaintiff had to prove that the defendant was in possession of the thing and could produce it. If he succeeded in proving this and the defendant refused to produce the thing, he would be sentenced to pay an amount of money.

A further application of the action was against a person who *mala fide* dispossessed himself in order to frustrate the claim against him.

17. Reivindicatio

The *reivindicatio* was the *actio in rem* from the *ius civile* which action protected the *dominus ex iure Quiritium*. By way of this action the owner reclaimed possession from any person in possession of the thing without title against him, irrespective of whether the possessor was *bona fide* or *mala fide*.

In the *legisactio*-process the plaintiff made the formal claim *'Hunc ego hominem meum esse aio ex iure Quiritium . . .'* and the *intentio* of the *formula* read as follows *'Si paret rem de qua agitur A''A'' esse . . .'*. From both formulations it should be clear that the action was *in rem* and thus lay against anyone in whose possession the thing was found. The possessor had, however, to be in possession without title against the owner, which means that a pledger or a lessor could not make use of the *reivindicatio* to recover the pledged or leased thing, but has to claim with his *actio pigneraticia* or *actio locati*.

The *reivindicatio* was instituted against the person in possession of the thing, but the notion of possession underwent drastic changes in the course of Roman law. If for example B is the *bona fide possessor* of A's object and he (B) lets this object to C; against whom does A institute the *reivindicatio?* against B the lessor, who is the *possessor* or against C the lessee, who is the *detentor?*

FICTI POSSESSORES

In Justinian law the *reivindicatio* could also be instituted against so-called *ficti possessores*. This term denotes persons who were not in possession either because they had dispossessed themselves fraudulently in order to escape the *reivindicatio* or defendants who defended the action while not in possession of the object. These *ficti possessores* were sentenced to pay a sum of money.

The owner who was not in possession instituted the *reivindicatio* against the possessor who was not the owner. The action purported to establish the ownership of the plaintiff and condemnation of the defendant. This condemnation was always for money, cf the *condemnatio pecuniaria* of the *formula*, the direction to the judge to condemn the defendant to a sum of money. Therefore, a *clausula arbitraria* appeared in the *formula* of the *reivindicatio* which gave the defendant the option of returning the thing in issue and be absolved.

The plaintiff had to prove his ownership and where he succeeded the judge condemned the defendant to a sum of money unless he had restored the thing. The judge had to assess the amount in question and had to take the so-called *causa rei* into consideration. *Causa rei* included fruits, damages and expenses while the distinction between *bona fide* and *mala fide* possessors determined exactly what could be claimed. The *bona fide* possessor was liable for the *fructus extantes* before *litiscontestatio* and all fruits after *litiscontestatio*, for intentional damage before and intentional and negligent damages after *litiscontestatio*.

The *mala fide* possessor was liable for all fruits and all intentional or negligent damages. In Justinian law both the *bona fide* and the *mala fide* possessor had an action for compensation of *impensae necessariae*, necessary expenses, and *impensae utiles*, useful expenses. Both had a *ius tollendi* provided that they could exercise this right without causing harm and the removal was not useless.

18. Actio publiciana

Actio Publiciana was the *actio in rem* granted by the *praetor* to the person who received a *res mancipi* informally by way of *traditio*.

This action gave exactly the same protection as the *reivindicatio* of the *dominus ex iure Quiritium*. By way of this action the praetorian or bonitary owner reclaimed possession during the term of prescription from any person in possession of the thing without title against him, irrespective of whether the possessor was *bona fide* or *mala fide*.

Since *mancipatio, in iure cessio* and the distinction between *res mancipi* and *res nec mancipi* became obsolete during the post-classical period to so-called praetorian ownership disappeared as well.

In Justinian law, however, a new application for the *actio Publiciana* was created, namely the protection of the *possessor ad usucapionem*, the person usucaping. Thus, anybody who had acquired a *res habilis ex iusta causa bona fide* from a *non-dominus* could during the period of *usucapio* institute the *actio Publiciana* against any person in possession of the thing without title against him, irrespective of whether the possessor was *bona fide* or *mala fide*, except against the dominus.

19. Possession

In everyday speech possession and ownership are often used as synonyms, because most owners are in possession of their property. Legally there is, however, an important distinction between the two concepts. For example the *reivindicatio* was instituted by the owner, who had lost possession, against the possessor, who was not owner; this possessor could become owner by means of *usucapio*.

Ownership is a right. Possession is a factual situation, namely the physical control of a corporeal object. Possession is, in essence, a factual, corporeal relation with a thing. It should be noted that the physical control of a small movable is easier to comprehend than physical control of large movables and immovables. Nevertheless, though possession is essentially a factual relation it plays an important part in the law. Possession is the foundation of the system of ownership, since it is in most cases possession plus another legal fact that led to *dominium*. For example possession plus time created *dominium* by way of *usucapio;* possession plus *res nullius* created *dominium* by way of *occupatio;* possession plus *iusta causa* created *dominium* or bonitary ownership by way of *traditio*. In short most methods of acquisition of ownership are founded on the possession of the thing. Secondly, possession came to be protected in itself by praetorian remedies, namely *interdicta*, and in some cases even possession which was not rightfully acquired was protected by the *praetor*.

This brings us to the obvious question, why did the *praetor* protect possession? The answer is partly found in historical reasons and partly in public policy.

The historical reasons were firstly that the ownership of the *ager publicus*, public land in Italy, was vested in the Roman people during the republic. In other words this land was not held in private ownership and the holders of public land who had the use and enjoyment, could not institute the *reivindicatio* when they lost possession. Secondly, there was an aspect which was important in litigation, namely the fact that the defendant in possession of the object had the advantage in a *reivindicatio*. Therefore, one had to be prevented from taking matters into one's own hands in order to ensure this advantage.

Finally, some parties deserved protection and before the right in question had fully developed the *praetor* granted protection by way of an interdict, for example the pledgee.

The other reason for the protection of possession is one of public policy. It appears as if the possessor has a right; he is for appearance sake in the same position, in relation to the object, as the owner. Third parties have to respect this relationship and cannot take matters into their own hands, but have to take legal steps. It is for this very reason that possession was and is protected until due legal process has taken place. Thus, the *status quo* is protected for the time being. This point of view is expressed by the maxim *Qualiscumque enim possessor hoc ipso quod possessor est, plus iuris habet quam ille qui non possidet*, irrespective of type the possessor has by virtue of his being a possessor a greater right than somebody who does not possess.

Possessory protection appeared early during the republican period. A possessor whose possession was threatened or who had lost possession, approached the *praetor* and asked for an interdict. The *praetor* investigated the *causa possessionis*, the title of his possession, and granted or refused the interdict on an *ad hoc* basis.

Towards the end of the republic the *ager publicus* became private land and the jurists started their attempts to construe a theory with regard to the granting of interdictal protection to some possessors and not to others.

The starting point of the Roman jurists of the classical period, was the distinction between protected and unprotected possession. The real problem was to ascertain on what principle interdictal protection was granted. The characteristics of protected possession were that the person had physical control over the thing and used it as his own. Therefore, protected possession had to have two elements, namely *corpus*, the physical control, which became an elastic concept largely dependant on what was accepted in the community as physical control and secondly the *animus domini*, the intention to hold the thing as an owner.

Although the classical terminology was not uniform, but rather unclear and disturbing, it is common to distinguish the following types of possession: *possessio civilis, possessio ad interdicta* and *possessio naturalis.*

POSSESSIO CIVILIS

Possessio civilis or *possessio ad usucapionem* was the protected physical control which, through *usucapio*, could lead to *dominium.* This meant that the person who acquired a *res mancipi* informally by way of *traditio* from the owner as well as the person who acquired as *res habilis bona fide ex iusta causa* from a *non-dominus* fell within this category. Both had acquired physical control over the thing on the basis of a *iusta causa* and both had the *animus domini.* Both usucapers were protected by interdicts and in due course by the *actio publiciana.*

POSSESSIO AD INTERDICTA

This second group of protected possessors included in the first place the owner, the *bona fide possessor* not capable of *usucapio* and the *mala fide possessor.* All these had physical control over the thing, as well as the *animus domini.*

Interdicts for the protection of their possession were, however, granted to the following possessors, the *emphytenticarius, superficiarius*, pledgee, *precario tenens* and *sequester.* This possessory protection is difficult to explain on the basis of theoretical principles and must, therefore, have been inspired by practical necessity.

POSSESSIO NATURALIS

The final category of *possessio naturalis* or *detentio*, detention, denoted the unprotected possession of persons who had physical control of a thing, but could not seek the protection of the interdicts.

The *detentor* exercised the physical control on behalf of someone else and thus did not have the necessary *animus domini*. If, therefore, the *detentor* were deprived of the physical control, it was the person from whom he held who was entitled to the interdict. For example the lessee was a *detentor* and the lessor was granted the interdict on the argument that the lessor possessed by way of the lessee. In post-classical law the original premise that possession is merely a factual relation was gradually relinquished as the *animus domini*-element of protected possession was stressed and the *corpus*-element blurred. Consequently, a person could retain possession *animo solo* even if in fact physical control of the thing had been lost and possession came to be regarded as a right, the so-called *ius possessionis* and no longer merely as a factual relation.

20. Acquisition, retention and loss of possession

The two characteristic elements of protected possession were *corpus* and *animus* and consequently in classical law both elements were essential for the acquisition of protected possession. The acquisition of physical control of the thing with the intention to hold it as an owner provided the protection of the interdicts.

Protected possession would be retained as long as the possessor exercised physical control with the required *animus* and would be lost as soon as one or both of the essential elements disappeared. In post-classical law, however, possession could be retained *animo solo*, since greater prominence was given to *animus*.

ACQUISITION AND RETENTION OF POSSESSION THROUGH THIRD PARTIES

Although agency was in principle not recognized by Roman law, certain exceptions were gradually introduced. This was the case regarding acquisition of possession by the *paterfamilias* through persons in his *potestas*, the *procurator* could acquire possession for his principal and the *tutor* and *curator* could acquire possession for the *pupillus* and the *furiosus*.

Similarly, possession could be retained through a person *in potestate*, but this was extended to many other representatives, such as a lessee, a depositee, a borrower and other detentors.

21. Protection of possession

Possessory protection was achieved by interdicts. The person entitled to interdictal protection had to approach the *praetor* and claim the interdict.

Possessory interdicts were divided into the following categories: *interdicta adipiscendae possessionis*, interdicts to obtain possession, *interdicta retinendae possessionis*, interdicts to retain possession, and *interdicta recuperandae possessionis*, interdicts to regain possession. The interdicts to retain possession were also called *interdicta prohibitoria*, prohibitory interdicts, because they prohibited a person to disturb another's possession, while the interdicts to regain possession were also called *interdicta restitutoria*, restitutory interdicts, since they commanded a person to restore possession. The same interdict can, depending on the circumstances, be either prohibitory or restitutory.

The most important possessory interdicts were the *interdictum Uti possidetis* in respect of immovables and the *interdictum Utrubi*, for movables.

UTI POSSIDETIS

The *interdictum Uti possidetis* protected the present possessor of immovable property against any disturbance of his possession and the interdict was prohibitory in this instance. If however, the present possessor had obtained that possession *vi aut clam aut precario ab altero*, by force, secretly or by request from the other party, then this other party was entitled to the interdict even though he was not in possession. In this instance, the interdict was restitutory, as the present possessor was commanded to return possession to the person from whom he had obtained that possession *vi aut clam aut precario.*

UTRUBI

The *interdictum Utrubi* protected the party who had been in possession as against his opponent for the longest period during the past year. This could be, but was not necessarily the present possessor. Moreover, if the party who had held the thing for the greater part of the past year had obtained that possession *vi aut clam aut precario ab altero*, then this other party was entitled to the interdict. The interdict was, depending on the circumstances prohibitory or restitutory. Justinian changed the requirements in order to assimilate the two interdicts, so that *Utrubi* protected the present possessor of movables, unless his possession had been obtained *vi aut clam aut precario ab altero.*

UNDE VI

Finally, the *interdictum Unde vi* restored the possession of immovables lost by force and was, therefore, solely restitutory. This interdict had to be claimed within a year.

22. Servitudes

Servitudes are the first group of the *iura in re aliena*, rights over someone else's property. They entitle one person to use another's property to a greater or lesser degree. His right is protected by an *actio in rem*, which means that the holder of such a right can institute his action against anybody who infringes upon his right and the whole world has, therefore, to respect his right. Thus, if the owner of the object in which the servitude, or any other real right, is vested, dies and the ownership of the object devolves on the heir, or if the owner transfers the ownership of the object in question, this does not affect the real right in any way and the holder of the real right can enforce his right against the new owner of the object.

The two classes of servitudes are *servitutes rerum* or *praediales* or *reales*, the real or praedial servitutes, and *servitudes personarum* or *personales*, the personal servitudes. The last group are, however, real rights.

23. Praedial servitudes

Praedial servitudes are real rights over another's land for the benefit of the owner of adjacent land. The purpose of praedial servitudes is *fundus fundo servit*, the one piece of land serves the other piece of land.

It is to be stressed that servitudes adhere to the plots, hence the expressions *fundus* or *praedium serviens*, the servient plot and *fundus* or *praedium dominans*, the dominant tract of land. The relation between the two plots is *servitus*, which implies a burden on the one piece of land irrespective of the ownership and a benefit for the other piece of land, irrespective of the ownership. Servitudes, therefore, belong to the holder, in his capacity as the owner of the dominant tenement and burden the owner of the servient tenement in his capacity as the owner of that piece of land. As soon as these parties transfer their ownership, these parties are no longer affected by the servitude, but the servitude continues in favour of the new owner of the dominant plot and against the new owner of the servient plot.

The praedial servitudes can be sub-classified into *iura praediorum rusticorum*, rural praedial servitudes, and *iura praediorum urbanorum*, urban praedial servitudes.

The basis of this distinction is difficult to explain, but it would seem that urban servitudes were constituted for buildings.

24. Rural praedial servitudes

Rural servitudes were the oldest, since Rome was originally an agricultural society. Economic exploitation of a farming unit introduced the necessity of ceding certain right's to one's neighbour and the underlying principle was, and still is, that the benefit for the one farm should outweigh the burden on the other farm. Romans sold, donated, bequeathed rural servitudes to each other. It was, however, necessary to constitute the servitudes as real rights in order that subsequent owners of the plots in question would be bound, since personal rights are only enforceable against a particular person. The rural servitudes were *res manicipi* and were originally considered physical things for example one owned the pathway.

At a later stage servitudes were recognized as the earliest *res incorporales*, i.e. the right of passage instead of ownership of the pathway. Examples of rural servitudes were: *iter*, right of footpath, *actus*, right of driving cattle, *via*, right of driving vehicles, *aquaeductus*, right of leading water, *aquaehaustus*, right of drawing water, *ius pascendi*, right of grazing cattle, *ius pecoris ad aquam adpulsum*, right of driving cattle to water, *ius calcis coquendae*, right to dig and burn lime, *ius harena fodiendae*, right to take sand on, across or over the servient land.

25. Urban praedial servitudes

The urban servitudes were of a later date and the result of urbanization. These were classified as *res nec mancipi* as well as *res incorporales*.

Examples of urban servitudes were: *servitus oneris ferendi*, right of support of buildings, *servitus tigni inmittendi*, right of insertion of beams, *servitus altius non tollendi*, restriction on the height of buildings, *servitus fluminis recipiendi*, right to discharge running water through a gutter, *servitus stillicidii recipiendi*, right to discharge rain water, *servitus proiciendi protegendive*, right of projection of part of a building over the servient tenement, *servitus cloacae mittendae*, right to have a sewer running through the servient tenement, *servitus ne luminibus officiatur*, right to prevent one's neighbour from obscuring one's light, *servitus ne prospectui officiatur*, right to prevent one's neighbour from obstructing one's view.

26. Requirements for praedial servitudes

The abovementioned servitudes are only examples and not a complete list of all servitudes, since it is possible to create new servitudes as the necessity arises. The Roman jurists developed certain requirements which praedial servitudes had to meet in order to eliminate situations where the burden would outweigh the benefit.

REQUIREMENTS FOR PRAEDIAL SERVITUDES

The first and most important requirement was formulated in the rule *servitutium non ea natura est, ut aliquid faciat quis, . . . sed ut aliquid patiatur aut non faciat*, the nature of servitudes is not such that someone has to do something, but that he has to allow something or refrain from doing something. The person in question is the owner of the servient land and an active duty of performance is not required of him, since this would restrict his freedom as a person. The exception to this rule is found in the *servitus oneris ferendi* where the servient owner has the duty to keep in repair the supporting wall.

From this rule a further classification of servitudes can be deducted, namely the distinction between positive and negative servitudes.

This distinction relates to the dominant owner in the sense that a positive servitude gives the owner of the dominant land a positive right to do something, while a negative servitude gives him a right with a negative content, for instance that his neighbour shall not interfere with his light, view etc.

A second requirement was *praedio utilitas*, which means that the servitude had to benefit the plot. In other words any owner of the dominant plot had to benefit by the servitude, not only a particular owner. This requirement also implies that there has to be a dominant plot and that the two plots have to be adjacent, the so-called *vicinitas*-requirement.

Furthermore, since servitudes exist for the benefit of the dominant land which is indefinitely durable, it follows that a servitude is, in principle, perpetual; i.e. *causa perpetua*. Consequently, a servitude cannot be constituted subject to a resolutive condition or term.

Furthermore, *nulli res sua servit*, which means that an owner of land cannot have a servitude over his own property, since a servitude is a *ius in re aliena*. This leads to the consequence that when the owner of one of the two plots acquires the ownership of the other plot, the servitude was terminated and did not revive if at a later stage the ownership of one of the two properties was transferred. A servitude had to be exercised *civiliter modo*, so as to cause the minimum of inconvenience.

Finally, the rules *servitus servitutis esse non potest*, there cannot be a servitude on another servitude, and the rule that a servitude is indivisible have to be mentioned.

27. Personal servitudes

Servitutes personales or *personarum*, personal servitudes are *iura in re aliena*, real rights over someone else's property. These servitudes belong to the holder in his personal capacity. In other words it is not necessary to be an owner of land to be the holder of a personal servitude. The personal servitudes have little in common with the praedial servitudes, except that both are real rights over another's property and their modes of constitution and termination were the same.

It must be stressed that the personal servitudes adhere to the person and are thus of limited duration, since they cease to exist on the death of that person. It is clear that the holder of a personal servitude cannot transfer the servitude to another as it inheres exclusively in his person, but the holder can grant the use of the right to another. For example, the usufructuary of a house can let the house, but cannot transfer the usufruct. Only four personal servitudes were recognized.

28. Usufructus

Usufructus, usufruct, developed as a means of providing for the widow without letting property go out of the family.

Usufructus est ius alienis rebus utendi fruendi salva rerum substantia, usufruct is the right to use and enjoy the things of another, retaining their substance.

It is clear that usufruct is a *ius in re aliena*, which may be constituted over immovables and over movables which are not consumed by use.

The *salva rerum substantia* requirement means, firstly, that the usufructuary was not entitled to affect the character of the object, for example opening a quarry on a farm. Secondly, the usufructuary had to maintain the property, for example the number of a herd or vines. Furthermore, as a result of the *salva rerum substantia* requirement only *res non consumptibiles*, things that are not consumed by normal use, can be the object of a usufruct.

The usufructuary had to use the property *civiliter modo* and was entitled to all fruits, i.e. *fructus naturales* and *fructus civiles*. *Perceptio*, gathering, of the natural fruits made him the owner thereof.

Since the usufructuary has the right to use the thing he necessarily has the thing in his possession. Although only a *detentor*, he was in classical law protected by a special interdict, the *interdictum quem usumfructum*, while Justinian granted him the general possessory interdicts. The owner of the usufructuary property has *nuda proprietas*, mere ownership, because the usufructuary has the *ius utendi fruendi*. The owner retains his *ius abutendi*, the right to transfer his ownership, but this does not affect the usufructuary's right, since he has a real right which he can assert against anyone, also against the new owner.

QUASI-USUFRUCTUS

Towards the beginning of the first century AD a *Senatus Consultum* provided that a usufruct of money was possible. The money should become the property of the usufructuary who had to give security by way of a *cautio usufructuaria* that a return of a similar amount of money would be made at the termination of the usufruct. Gradually the same principle was applied to other consumptibles and eventually even to *res incorporales*. The jurists called it *quasi-usufructus*.

29. Usus, habitatio and operae servorum vel animalium

Usus, use, was the real right to use another's property without having the fruits thereof. At a later stage the usuary was allowed to take fruits for his personal, daily needs. He had to use the thing *civiliter* and *salva rerum substantia*.

The *usuarius* was a *detentor*, but could assert his real right against anyone.

Habitatio, inhabitation, was the real right to live in another's house. He had to exercise his right *civiliter* and *salva rerum substantia*. Justinian allowed the *habitator* to let the house, thus differing from *usus*.

Operae servorum vel animalium was the real right to the services of another's slaves or animals.

30. Constitution of servitudes

Servitudes are real rights and as such have to be acquired in a certain manner. The agreement between the parties did not constitute a servitude, but was the reason for the actual legal act whereby the servitude is constituted.

METHODS BY WHICH SERVITUDES COULD BE CREATED

Mancipatio

Rural servitudes over Italic land were *res mancipi* and could consequently be constituted by *mancipatio* in favour of the owner of the dominant plot. This method became obsolete in post-classical law and was formally abolished by Justinian.

In iure cessio

Any servitude could be created by *in iure cessio*, which provided the necessary publicity, but the formalities were rather cumbersome. This method became obsolete as well.

Deductio servitutis

A further mode of constituting a servitude was *deductio servitutis*, reservation of a servitude in his own favour by a *dominus* mancipating part of his property. In later law this could be done as the transferor transferred part of his property by *traditio*.

Quasi traditio

Traditio of a servitude was, of course, impossible, since *traditio* is, in essence the transfer of possession, i.e. the physical control of a corporeal thing, servitudes being *res incorporales*.

The following practice developed, however: two parties agreed that the one would grant a servitude over his property to the other; the latter would exercise his 'right', so-called *usus*, and the other allowed him to do so, *patientia*. This situation, namely *usus* and *patientia*, was construed as a type of possession, *quasi possessio* and consequently the idea of *quasi traditio* became accepted. In principle *quasi traditio* would not create a real right, in that third parties were under no obligation to respect a 'servitude' constituted in this manner, but the *praetor* granted the holder an *actio in factum in rem*.

Pactiones atque stipulationes

The most important method used in later times, originated in the provinces, namely *pactiones atque stipulationes*. Since provincial land could not be owned by the individual, servitudes over such land could not be created by *mancipatio* or *in iure cessio*. The possessors of provincial land would come to an informal agreement, *pactio* or *pactum*, to grant a servitude, which was made enforceable by a *stipulatio*, the formal verbal contract of Roman law. This would, however, merely create a personal right against the party to the *stipulatio* and his heirs, but it seems that in respect of provincial land a right so created was given the relevant *actio in rem*.

This method was adopted in Rome and in Justinian law was the normal method of creating servitudes.

Legacy

A servitude could also be created by will in which the servitude was left as a legacy; this applied mainly to usufruct.

Prescription

Finally, prescription could give title to a servitude. Although the *Lex Scribonia* abolished acquisitive prescription of servitudes in the late Republic, in late classical law exercise, *usus* or *quasi possessio*, of ten years *inter praesentes* or twenty years *inter absentes*, gave a right *in rem*.

31. Termination of servitudes

Personal servitudes were terminated by the death of the holder. They would also end with *capitis deminutio maxima*, loss of liberty, and *capitis deminutio media*, loss of citizenship of the holder.

Furthermore, the personal servitudes would end with the arrival of the day, or the fulfilment of the condition, pending on which the servitude was established.

All servitudes were terminated by destruction of the thing; if the holder of the servitude became owner of the object in question, e.g. *nulli res sua servit*, by renunciation and extinctive prescription. A servitude had to be exercised to be preserved and non-use ended the right. Under Justinian the periods were three years in respect of movables and ten years *inter praesentes* and twenty years *inter absentes* in respect of immovables.

The distinction between positive and negative servitudes led to a difference regarding the requisite of non-use. For positive servitudes, it was enough that the holder did not exercise his right, but in the case of negative servitudes it was necessary for the servient owner to have acted contrary to the servitude and that the dominant owner had not acted against him during the relevant period.

32. Protection of servitudes

It is clear that servitudes are protected by an *actio in rem*, namely the *vindicatio servitutis*, an *actio in rem* which the holder could institute against anyone infringing on his servitude. The purpose of this action was to assert the plaintiff's servitude and to end the infringement. Justinian renamed this action *actio confessoria*.

Several servitudes were protected by special interdicts, for instance the *interdictum quem usumfructum* while for the others the *interdictum uti possidetis utilis* was granted.

33. Emphyteusis and superficies

Emphyteusis and *superficies* form a group apart. Both were *iura in re aliena*, real rights on another's property. The property in question was land and belonged to the state or to a city. Although these rights belonged to the holder in his personal capacity, they did not end with his death, but lasted, in principle, for as long as the yearly rent, *vectigal* or *canon* and *solarium*, was paid.

EMPHYTEUSIS

During the republican and classical period the institution of *ager vectigalis* was known, whereby a city or municipality let land *in perpetuum*, forever, to an individual as long as he paid the yearly *vectigal*, i.e. rent. The holder could use and enjoy the land, acquire fruits from the land, he could mortgage the land, create servitudes over it, dispose of it by will, sell it etc. Thus, he had most of the advantages of ownership. The yearly groundrent differed little from landtax and since the holder was protected by interdicts and an *actio in rem*, his position differed little in practical effect from that of an owner. In consequence, controversy arose whether this rights was constituted by the contract of sale, or by the contract of lease. In the provinces of Northern Africa a similar institution developed during the third century AD. The emperors let tracts of uncultivated land for long periods with the understanding that the land would be cultivated. This aspect is found in the name of this insitution, *emphyteusis*, to plant.

The two institutions merged and the yearly groundrent was known as *canon*. The emperor Zeno ruled, in the fifth century AD, that the right is not created by a contract of sale or lease, but by a contract *sui generis*, namely the *contractus emphyteuticarius*.

SUPERFICIES

Superficies is the real right to erect a building on another's land and to use it against payment of a yearly rent, *solarium*. As a rule the land belonged to the state or to a city, but it was used among private citizens as well. This right developed as a result of the need of town development and the principle of *superficies solo cedit*. The building became the property of the owner of the ground, but the *superficiarius* had the use and enjoyment of the building for as long as he paid the *solarium*. The *superficiarius* was protected by an interdict and an *actio in rem*.

34. Real security

When someone desires credit in many instances, this will only be granted if security for the performance of the debt is provided.

Security can be either real or personal. Personal security or suretyship takes place when another party, the surety, is personally liable to the creditor for the discharge of the debt.

Real security is when the debtor or a third party offer an object over which a real right in favour of the creditor is vested.

The real security rights are accessory to the obligation they secure. This means that the relationship between a creditor and a debtor is a prerequisite for their formation and existence. The holder of real security does not intend to use and enjoy the secured property, but desires security so that the debt will be discharged.

In the course of Roman legal development, there were three forms of real security, *fiducia, pignus* and *hypotheca*.

35. Fiducia

Fiducia was the earliest form of real security and stemmed from the *ius civile*. This constituted the most important form of real security during the republican and classical periods. Originally only *res mancipi*, but later all corporeal objects, could be used for *fiducia*. Created by *mancipatio* or *in iure cessio* it thus became obsolete in post-classical law.

Fiducia was constituted when the debtor (or another) transferred ownership by *mancipatio* (or *in iure cessio*) to the creditor as security for the discharge of his debt. Before or during the transfer of ownership, agreement was reached that the creditor would reconvey the ownership when the debt was discharged. This agreement, the *pactum fiduciae*, was originally not enforceable and the debtor was relying upon the *fiducia*, the trustworthiness, of the creditor. Fairly early the *praetor* granted a personal action, the *actio fiduciae*, to the debtor to enforce the *pactum fiduciae* against the creditor. In the *pactum fiduciae* all particulars were settled, the most important of which were the questions as to which party would have the use of the secured object and what would happen if the debt was not discharged. With regard to the last problem there were two standard agreements. Firstly, the so-called *lex commissoria* according to which the ownership of the secured object remained with the creditor, but without the limitations of the *pactum fiduciae*. The *pactum distrahendi*, the agreement that if the debt was not paid by an agreed date, the creditor should be entitled to sell the secured object.

It should be noted that the creditor did not acquire a *ius in re aliena*, but the *ius in re propria*, namely ownership. This made his position extremely favourable and consequently *fiducia* remained popular for a long time.

Fiducia was created by *mancipatio* or *in iure cessio* and *res mancipi* and later all corporeal things could be used for *fiducia*.

36. Pignus

Although it was not recognized by the *ius civile, pignus* was used quite early in everyday practice, in view of the factual power it gave the creditor. In due course the *praetor* recognized *pignus* as a second mode of real security by granting the pledgee protection by way of interdicts and finally an *actio in rem*. *Pignus* or pledge takes place when the debtor (or another) delivers the possession of a thing to the creditor as security for the discharge of a debt. The delivery is accompanied by an agreement of the parties that the thing will be given back when the debtor discharges his debt. This *pactum* accompanied by delivery, constitutes the contract of pledge. From this contract the debtor of the capital debt, i.e. the pledgor had a personal action, the *actio pigneraticia* against the pledgee for restoration of possession when the debt was discharged. The pledgor could institute the *reivindicatio*, against third parties in possession of the pledged object if he were the owner of the thing.

The creditor of the capital debt, i.e. the pledgee, had possession of the pledged thing. His possession was protected by the possessory interdicts as well as the *actio Serviana* or *actio quasi Serviana*. By means of this action, the pledgee could claim the possession of the pledged object from any person.

The pledgee had only a *ius possidendi*, a right to possess the pledged object. In principle he was not allowed to use or alienate the pledged thing, as this would be *furtum*. However, it became customary to reach various agreements regarding use and foreclosure.

PACTUM ANTICHRESEOS OR ANTICHRESIS

The agreement by which the pledgee could use the object as a type of interest on the capital debt.

PACTUM COMMISSORIUM OR LEX COMMISSORIA

The parties agreed that, if the principal obligation was not performed, the pledgee would become the owner of the pledge. This agreement had unacceptable implications, in that the creditor got excessive interest since the pledge is, as a rule, more valuable than the amount of the debt. Consequently, Constantine prohibited the *lex commissoria* in the fourth century AD.

PACTUM DISTRAHENDI

In this case the parties agreed that if the debt was not paid by an agree date, the pledgee should be entitled to sell the pledge. From the proceeds he then satisfied his claim and the *superfluum*, the excess had to be restored to the pledgor. This *pactum* developed during the classical period into a *ius distrahendi*, an implied right to sell the pledge, if the debt was not discharged. Justinian introduced a system of safeguards in relation to the *ius distrahendi.*

Pignus was created by *traditio* and all corporeal things could be used for *pignus.*

37. Hypotheca

The Roman lawyers did not make a distinction between *pignus* and *hypotheca*, since the latter developed as a modification of *pignus.*

Hypotheca was constituted when the debtor granted the creditor a real right in a thing as security for the discharge of a debt. This means that the creditor/pledgee could claim possession of the thing by means of an *actio in rem* from any person, if the debt was not paid. Once he had acquired possession of the object, he was in the same position as a pledgee, which means that the rules of *pignus* became applicable and more specific the *ius distrahendi* became operative. *Hypotheca* was, therefore, postponed *pignus* or *pignus* without possession. It should be stressed that in the case of *hypotheca* neither ownership nor possession of the pledged object was transferred; the debtor retained ownership as well as possession of the thing hypothecated to secure an obligation.

ORIGIN AND DEVELOPMENT OF HYPOTHECA

Hypotheca originated from a practice in the leasing of land. The landowner desired security for the payment of the rent, but the tenant had only movables, such as cattle, slaves, agricultural implements, which he needed to exploit the farm. Therefore, the landowner and the tenant agreed that the tenant's *invecta et illata*, the movables which he brought on the leased property, would serve as security for the payment of the rent. This agreement was, however, a mere *pactum* and thus unenforceable.

The *praetor* eventually made this *pactum* enforceable by granting the landowner an interdict, the *interdictum Salvianum*, against the tenant. This means that the landowner could obtain possession of the *invecta et illata* from the tenant once the rent was due, but unpaid. This interdict could, however, only be used against the tenant and not against third parties and did thus not grant real security.

Next, the *praetor* granted a real action, the *actio Serviana*, to the landowner. By way of this action he could obtain possession of the *invecta et illata* from any person, thus giving him a real right in the *invecta et illata*. Once he had obtained possession of the *invecta et illata* he could exercise the *ius distrahendi*.

Finally, *hypotheca* was extended to create a security over any form of *res*, this means that in all cases where a debtor-creditor relationship existed and the debtor required security for the performance, anything could be used for *hypotheca*. The action in these cases was the *actio quasi Serviana*, later called the *actio hypothecaria*.

FORMATION OF HYPOTHECA

Firstly *hypotheca* could be created by means of a *pactum*. The creditor and the debtor agreed informally that a certain thing or things would serve as security for the discharge of the debtor's debt.

The lack of formalities caused a lack of publicity with the inherent danger of swindling. The possibility of eviction by way of the *actio hypothecaria* had always to be taken into account by a new owner.

Secondly, a testator could state in his will that a certain thing or things in his estate were to serve as security for the payment of a legacy.

Finally, there were the so-called *hypothecae tacitae* or *legitimae*, tacit or legal hypothecs. In certain circumstances a creditor acquired a hypothec over a certain thing or over the whole estate of the debtor by operation of law, in short without any agreement between the parties in this respect. The most important examples of these were the tacit hypothec of the lessor over the property brought by the lessor onto the leased premises, *invecta et illata*, as security for payment of the rent; the *fiscus*, imperial fisc, had a tacit hypothec over the whole estate of its debtors, mainly in respect of taxes due to it; the ward had a tacit hypothec over his tutor's estate, the wife for her dowry over her husband's estate, the *legatarius* and *fideicommissarius* had tacit hypothecs over the estate of the heir as security for the payment of their legacy or *fideicommissum*.

One of the advantages of *hypotheca* was that virtually anything could be used for it, namely all things that could be sold, movables, immovables, corporeal and incorporeal things, existing as well as future *res*, individual things or a whole estate. The reason for this was found in the fact that the creditor was only interested in the *ius distrahendi* with the result that the only criterion which applied was whether the thing in question could be sold.

PRIOR TEMPORE, POTIOR IURE

There could be more than one *hypotheca* on the same thing, in other words the same thing could be hypothecated more than once at the same time to guarantee different obligations of different creditors. This was impossible in the cases of *fiducia* and *pignus*, since ownership and possession can only be transferred once. *Hypotheca* did not deprive the debtor of either ownership or possession as he only granted the creditor a real right in the object, while it is obvious that more than one real right could be vested in the same thing.

Therefore, it could easily happen that the total amount of the debts secured by hypothecs exceeded the value of the hypothecated thing. As a rule, the creditors would be unaware of this, because hypothecs were created informally, without publicity, by agreement and Roman law did not know registration of *hypothecae*.

The rule *prior tempore, potior iure*, determined which creditor would suffer the possible loss in these circumstances. The creditor whose *hypotheca* was created first, was the first to satisfy his claim from the proceeds of the sale of the hypothecated thing; the next one to satisfy his claim, was the second etc. This means that the creditors whose hypothecs came last, were the ones who suffered the possible loss. The *prior tempore, potior iure* rule was made effective by the fact that only the first secured creditor could exercise the *ius distrahendi*. Any secured creditor could, once his claim had become enforceable and was not met, obtain possession of the hypothecated thing by means of the *actio hypothecaria* from anybody, but only the first secured creditor could sell the thing. After the sale, the secured creditors were paid out according to *prior tempore, potior iure*.

EXCEPTIONS TO THE PRIOR TEMPORE, POTIOR IURE RULE

Certain tacit hypothecs were privileged, which put them at the top of the list even if they had originated later in time. Examples were the tacit hypothec of the *fiscus* and the wife.

In later law, hypothecs registered with the authorities, or effected in writing before three witnesses became privileged.

Furthermore, the *prior tempore, potior iure* rule could be bypassed by the *ius offerendi et succedendi*. A later creditor could offer to pay the debt due to an earlier creditor and in this way take his place for both debts.

38. Termination of real security

All forms of real security were extinguished by discharge of the debt which they secured. The real security rights were accessory to the principal debt and dissolution of this obligation extinguished them as well.

Another important way of ending these real rights, was the exercising of the *ius distrahendi*, if the debtor failed to repay the debt at the due date.

Furthermore destruction of the secured thing, merger through which the creditor became the owner of the thing in question, extinctive prescription, renunciation by the creditor and the *ius offerendi et succedendi* could also terminate real security.

CHAPTER IV – The law of obligations

The Romans classified the law of obligations as a part of the law of property, i.e. *ius quod ad res pertinet.* Today it is classified as a separate section of private law.

The Roman law of obligations forms the basis of the modern law of obligations in most western legal systems. However, the historical descendency and the consequent large degree of coincidence between the two can be misleading, since the same concept can have developed during twenty centuries of legal history and may have acquired a different content. Cf for example the *contractus* of Gaius, *contractus* of Justinian and our modern contract which each have a different meaning.

1. What is an obligation

Justinian gives the following definition: *Obligatio est iuris vinculum quo necessitate adstringimur alicuius solvendae rei, secundum nostrae civitatis iura.* An obligation is a legal bond whereby we are bound by the necessity of performing something according to the laws of our state.

It is possible to criticize this definition, however, it's importance is found in the fact it mentions the essence of an obligation, namely that *iuris vinculum,* legal bond.

A legal bond is an abstract bond recognized by the law, which binds two parties. The one party, the creditor, has a right, a personal right, against the other party, the debtor. This is obviously a personal right as it can be enforced only against that particular person.

Cf. *Dig* 44 7 3 pr (Paulus libro secundo institutionum). *Obligationum substantia non in eo consistit, ut aliquod corpus nostrum aut servitutem nostram faciat, sed ut alium nobis obstringat ad dandum aliquid vel faciendum vel praestandum.* The substance of obligations does not consist in giving us ownership of something or a servitude but in binding someone to use, to give, do or perform something.

The person who binds himself to someone else, places an obligation on himself only; in so doing he gives the creditor a right against himself, while third parties do not become involved. The creditor has a personal right which he enforces with a personal action, an *actio in personam,* against that particular debtor. The question arises as to what the creditor claims with his personal action, in other words what is the duty of the debtor?

According to Justinain: . . . *alicuius solvendae rei* . . .; while Paulus states that: . . . *ad dandum aliquid vel faciendum vel praestandum.* The debtor has to perform something for the creditor; in other words he must either give something to the creditor, do something for him or refrain from doing something. Within certain limits any act or omission can be the object of a performance. Thus an obligation is a legal bond whereby a debtor has a duty to perform towards a creditor and the creditor has a personal right against the debtor to enforce performance.

2. The origin and development of obligations

Obligatio and *actio in personam* are associated. According to the ancient law of legal redress an *actio in personam* was asserted and enforced by way of the *legisactio per sacramentum in personum*.

When a judge had given a decision in favour of a plaintiff, the defendant became *iudicatus*. If the *iudicatus* did not voluntarily satisfy the judgment debt, execution of the judgment could be obtained by way of the *legisactio per manus iniectionem*. *Manus iniectio* was the seizure of the person of the *iudicatus*, i.e. an *obligatus* against whom a judgment was obtained. This implies that *obligari*, to enter into an obligation, was an extremely important act in primitive Roman society.

Only a limited number of legal acts created obligations: (a) delicts like *furtum* and *iniuria*, where the victim had the right to seek revenge on the person of the perpetrator. (b) lawful acts in law like *nexum* and *sponsio*, where someone binds himself formally. The bondage was originally literal with physical subjection.

Gradually the Roman law of obligations accepted an increasing number of lawful acts as well as acts contrary to law as sources of obligations. The *praetor* introduced new *formulae*, i.e. more *actiones in personam* and consequently more obligations. Only the person against whom a personal action can be enforced is an *obligatus*, i.e. debtor.

3. Various classifications of obligations

The jurists began systematizing the law and the following classifications were recognized:

OBLIGATIO CIVILIS & OBLIGATIO HONORARIA

Obligatio civilis was an obligation which arose from sources recognized by the *ius civile*. This type of obligation was enforceable by an *actio civilis*, an action derived from the *ius civile*.

Obligatio honoraria was an obligation which arose from the *ius honorarium*. This type of obligation was redressed by an *actio honoraria*, an action created by the *praetor* or other magistrate.

OBLIGATIO CIVILIS & OBLIGATIO NATURALIS

Obligatio civilis (in a second and wider sense) was any obligation enforceable by means of an action.

Obligatio naturalis, natural obligation was a normal obligation which for special reasons was not enforceable by action; that is an action was refused or in the event of an action being granted, execution was not possible. In other respects a natural obligation was a normal obligation; such an obligation could be validly carried out by performance, could be guaranteed by personal or real security and qualified for *compensatio*, set-off, *novatio*, novation, and release by way of a *pactum*.

OBLIGATIO STRICTI IURIS & OBLIGATIO BONAE FIDEI

Obligatio stricti iuris was an obligation which arose from a legal act of the *strictum ius*, the strict and formal *ius civile*.

These obligations were enforced by an *actio civilis* and in such a case a judge was bound by the strict rules of the formal law.

Obligatio bonae fidei was an obligation which derived from an act of law based on the *bona fides*, good faith. These obligations were enforced by an *actio bonae fidei*. In the *formula* of this action the words *ex fide bona* appeared and consequently a judge had to take the requirements of good faith into consideration.

4. The sources of obligations

The question which comes to fore in this chapter is how an obligation arises between two parties? In other words, what legal act or legal fact created an obligation according to Roman law.

Gaius says in Inst 3 88 that *Omnis enim obligatio vel ex contractu nascitur vel ex delicto*, every obligation arises either from contract of from delict.

This suggests, that all obligations arose, either from a lawful legal act, or from a wrongful act. However, the majority of lawful legal acts which created obligations, were transacted because there was agreement or consent on the part of the parties to bring an obligation about. Therefore, at a later stage the concept of a contract was refined and it was recognized, that agreement was of the essence of a contract. Consequently the term *contractus* signified in later law a legal act based on the *consensus*, agreement, by the parties to create an obligation. Gaius' dichotomy of the sources of the obligation therefore became unsatisfactory, since an obligation could also arise from a legal act to which there was no agreement on the part of the parties.

Accordingly a third source of obligations is mentioned, the *Res Cottidianae*, attributed to Gaius in the Digest : D 44 7 1 pr *Obligationes aut ex contractu nascuntur aut ex maleficio aut proprio quodam iure ex variis causarum figuris*, obligations arise from contract, from delict or by some provision of law from various types of cause. In this context, *contractus* connotes a legal act based on the *consensus* by the parties to create an obligation; *variae causarum figurae* refers to legal acts not based on agreement but which were lawful, while *maleficium* is the equivalent of *delictum*.

In Justinian's Institutes a fourfold division of the sources of obligations is found.

Inst 3 13 2 : *aut enim ex contractu sunt aut quasi ex contractu aut ex maleficio aut quasi ex maleficio*, for obligations arise from contract or as if from contract, from delict or as if from delict. While the terms *contractus* and *maleficium* confirm the descriptions of contract and delict given above, two new categories were introduced viz quasi-contract and quasi-delict. The concept quasi-contract denotes those lawful acts not founded on agreement which constitute an obligation, while the notion quasi-delict does not differ substantially from the category of delict.

5. Contractus

As has been said, by high classical law, contract signified a legal act based on the *consensus* by the parties to create an obligation.

However, this does not imply that every agreement whereby a person undertakes performance towards another party gave rise to an obligation.

In Roman law an agreement between two parties only gave rise to an obligation if the agreement could be classified, on the basis of its form or content, into one of the categories according to which the Roman law recognized an *actio in personam*. *Consensus* as such, created a *pactum, pactio* or *conventio*, a pact between the parties. *Ex nudo pacto non oritur actio*, a mere pact does not give rise to an action viz obligation.

In order to be enforceable as a *contractus* there was the further requirement that the agreement should have an additional element. This further element was referred to as the *causa contractus*. The law recognized four *causae* and consequently a fourfold classification of *contractus* is found.

1. *Contractus re*, contracts which were constituted by agreement and the transfer of a thing.
2. *Contractus verbis*, contracts which were constituted by agreement and the use of formal words.
3. *Contractus litteris*, contracts which were constituted by agreement and formal writing.

4. *Contractus consensu*, contracts constituted by mere agreement.
Although the last category forms an exception to the abovementioned system of the Roman law, only four contracts were concluded by simple agreement by the parties.

Moreover, in each category a limited number of agreements, combined with the *causa* formed a contract and gave rise to an obligation or obligations. Consequently, in Roman law the number of contracts was limited.

6. Other classifications of contracts and quasi-contracts

Contracts and quasi-contracts can also be classified as follows:

Unilateral (quasi-) contract is a (quasi-) contract which gives rise to only one obligation. In other words, only one duty is imposed on one of the contracting parties, while the other party, the creditor, has a personal right correlative to the duty involved against the debtor.

Bilateral or synallagmatic (quasi-) contract is a (quasi-) contract which gives rise to two obligations. These (quasi-) contracts impose duties on both the contracting parties. Both parties have personal rights correlative to the duties involved against each other. The aim of these contracts is an exchange of performances.

Imperfectly bilateral (quasi-) contract is a (quasi-) contract which in principle gives rise to only one obligation. However, it is possible for a counter claim to arise, which is enforced by an *actio contraria*.

7. The content of contracts

Within certain limits any act or omission could be the object of a performance, i.e. the content of a contract.

The requirements for a valid performance were the following:

- *(a)* Performance must not be contrary to the law or the *boni mores*, public morals.
- *(b)* Performance must be definable.
- *(c)* Performance must be appraisable in money.
- *(d)* Performance must be in favour of the contracting creditor. A contractual agreement for a performance in favour of a third party was in principle void.
- *(e)* The performance must be possible.

The debtor was bound to do something or to refrain from doing something and the words *dare, facere* and *praestare* are used to denote the type of performance.

Dare was to transfer *dominium iure Quiritium*, ownership recognized by the *ius civile*, but was also used in a wide sense of giving.

Facere was to do something and also encompassed refraining from doing something.

Praestare originally meant to bind oneself as surety but was generally used in the wider sense of performing.

The performance can be *certum*, specific or *incertum*, not specific.

Obligatio alternativa. In this case performance was alternative, in other words one or another performance was due, but the creditor was entitled to only one performance. As a rule the debtor could choose which performance to deliver.

Obligatio facultativa, the performance was factultative; only one performance was due but the debtor was entitled to perform another specific performance in place of the original performance.

Performance can be generic i.e. the object of performance is specified according to type. *Genera non pereunt* the type does not disappear, even if the thing in question perishes, the obligation to perform continues.

8. Possibility of performance

If performance is physically or legally impossible, the general rule in Roman law was *impossibilium nulla obligatio est*, there is no obligation for the impossible. The test for impossibility was objective: subjective impossibility, in other words, where the performance would have been possible for another, was irrelevant.

Generic performance is never objectively impossible, for *genera non pereunt.*

With regard to impossibility, an important distinction must be made between initial impossibility and supervening impossibility.

Initial impossibility i.e. where performance was already impossible at the time of the conclusion of the contract. The *impossibilium*-rule applies in general and the obligation to this rule was found with regard to the *negotia bonae fidei*, legal acts based on good faith, if the debtor was aware of the impossibility; he then acted contrary to good faith and was liable for damages.

Supervening impossibility, i.e. where performance was possible at the time of the conclusion of the contract, but was rendered impossible by subsequent events.

In this case a valid obligation has arisen but before the duty arising from the obligation could be fulfilled, performance became impossible.

The Roman law principle of *impossibilum nulla obligatio est iura* was applicable in this instance as well.

It follows from this that the debtor is released from his obligation to perform and the risk for supervening impossibility is borne by the creditor. However, this can lead to unjust consequences vis à vis the creditor, since performance can become impossible in various ways:

(a) The debtor can cause impossibility intentionally.

(b) Impossibility can occur as a result of the debtor's negligence.

(c) Performance can become impossible through *casus fortuitus*, accident.

(d) Impossibility of performance can be caused by *vis major*, an act of God.

It would have been unjust to release the debtor from his duty in all these cases and consequently Roman law developed a number of exceptions to the *impossibilium*-rule. The practical implication of this was that in certain instances impossibility of performance did not release the debtor from his obligation to perform, but that the creditor could still institute his personal action derived from their contract. With this action he claimed either the pecuniary value of the impossible performance or damages depending on the kind of contract.

Under these circumstances the debtor was liable.

9. Contractual liability

The distinction between the *negotia stricti iuris* and the *negotia bonae fidei* played an important part in this regard.

NEGOTIA STRICTI IURIS

Stipulatio, the most important of Roman contracts, was a *negotium stricti iuris.*

In principle, the *impossibilium*-rule was applied without qualifications, i.e. the debtor was discharged from liability and thus the creditor did not have a claim for the pecuniary value of the performance. Consequently in pre-classical Roman law the custom developed of entering a clause in the contract, by which the debtor undertook that it would not be on his account that performance became impossible.

In later law this clause was implied, with the result that in spite of the fact that performance had become impossible the obligation remained in force, i.e. the debtor was still bound and the creditor could claim the pecuniary value of the impossible performance. This principle was formulated in two rules:

factum debitoris perpetuat obligationem, a positive act on the part of the debtor perpetuates the obligation, and

mora debitoris perpetuat obligationem, mora on the part of the debtor perpetuates the obligation.

NEGOTIA BONAE FIDEI

In these cases the debtor had the duty to perform *ex fide bona*, according to the requirements of good faith. This implied that if performance became impossible as the result of bad faith on the part of the debtor, he remained still bound, so *mala fides* made the debtor liable. Furthermore, in the discussion of each individual contract it will be noticed that a number of debtors were held liable even in cases where there was no question of *mala fides*.

The classical lawyers decided casuistically, from case to case, and only later an attempt was made to develop a general system.

A second distinction which has to be made in this context, is therefore, the division between classical law and the law of Justinian.

Contractual liability of debtors with regard to *negotia bonae fidei* in classical law.

(a) Since all debtors from *negotia bonae fides* had to perform *ex fide bona*, every one of them was held liable for *mala fides*. The concept used in this context was *dolus*, i.e. *dolus* in classical law was synonymous with *mala fides*, i.e. when one does not act according to the requirements of good faith.

(b) Secondly a number of debtors were held liable for impossibility of performance, even in cases where no *mala fides* on their part existed.
These debtors had a duty of *custodire*, safe keeping and the practical implication is, that they were held liable for everything except *vis major*, an act of God. The practical consequence in classical law was that these debtors were liable for their *mala fides* as well as for *casus fortuitus*, an accident; e.g. if performance became impossible because the thing in question was stolen and there was no negligence on the part of the debtor, the creditor nevertheless could institute an action for damages against the debtor.

Contractual liability of debtors with regard to *negotia bonae fidei* under the law of Justinian.

As a result of the influence of Greek philosophy on the one hand and Christianity on the other, the principle developed, that there should be no liability without negligence. This entailed that the liability for *custodia* had to disappear. In the *Corpus Juris Civilis* the standard of liability of each debtor is laid down by each contract. Unfortunately the terminology of the *Corpus Juris Civilis* is not very consistent: *dolus, culpa lata, culpa levis, omnis culpa, culpa, exactissima diligentia, diligentia quam suis rebus adhibere solet, culpa levis in concreto* etc. are used rather loosely.

The Justinian system distinguished the following degrees of contractual liability:

Dolus. In the Justinian law *dolus* denotes *dolus malus*, i.e. intentional or conscious wrongdoing. It is obvious, that all debtors were liable for this kind of *dolus*.

Culpa. This was meant to include any reprehensible conduct excluding *dolus*.

Three degrees of *culpa* were recognized in Justinian law:

(a) Culpa levis in abstracto. In this instance the debtor had to show the same

care, as a *bonus et diligens paterfamilias*, a diligent head of a family. Other expressions used in this context were *exactissima diligentia*, the highest degree of care, and *culpa levissima*, the slightest negligence. This degree of *culpa* implied that the debtors conduct was tested against an objective criterion, viz. how would a diligent head of a family have acted in similar circumstances?

Those debtors who were liable for *custodia* in classical law became liable for *culpa levis in abstracto* in later law.

(b) *Culpa levis in concreto*. The debtor had to show the same degree of care as he would show in his own affairs.

(c) *Culpa lata*, gross negligence, which for all practical purposes can be equated to *dolus*.

Therefore, as a rule, in cases of supervening impossibility, the basic principle of *impossibilium nulla obligatio est* applied i.e. the debtor was released from his obligation to perform. However, whether the specific debtor was indeed released from his obligation, depended firstly, on the circumstances under which performance had become impossible and secondly, on the liability of the debtor under the relevant contractual relationship. If a debtor was liable, the consequence was that the creditor could institute a personal action for damages based on the relevant contract.

10. Mora

Mora could be either *debitoris* or *creditoris*. *Mora debitoris* was when performance was due and possible but the debtor failed to perform due to his fault. This brings us to the question when performance is due. In principle, if there are no conditions or terms in the contract, the debtor is bound to perform immediately when the obligation arises. It is obvious that the debtor is not *in mora* immediately from the moment that the obligation arose but that it is necessary to take the circumstances of each particular case into consideration. In other words, it is a question of fact rather than of law.

Therefore in practice an *interpellatio* request, by the creditor was required to create *mora debitoris;* otherwise the debtor would not know that the creditor wanted performance and there would be no fault on his part.

Secondly, performance had to be possible, otherwise the *impossibilum*-rule and the question of the debtor's liability became operative, while *mora* applies where the debtor is in arrears with his performance. Such failure to perform has to be due to the fault of the debtor.

A distinction must be made between the case where the parties have agreed that performance is due before or on a certain day and cases where no such arrangement was made.

With regard to the first group the expression *mora ex re* is used and the debtor fell automatically into arrears with his performance, if he failed to honour his legal duty at the proper time. *Dies interpellat pro homine*, the day requests in the place of the man, which means that no request by the creditor was necessary before there could be *mora*.

If, however, no date for performance was set, the creditor had to request the debtor to fulfil his duty in order to achieve *mora debitoris* and the term *mora ex persona* is used to express this notion.

The consequences of *mora debitoris* are summed up in the rule *mora debitoris perpeluat obligationem*, the debtor's *mora* perpetuates the obligation.

This means, that if performance became impossible after the debtor was in *mora*, the obligation remained in force and the creditor could sue for a sum of money equal to the value of the performance. It was irrelevant in what way performance became impossible as the debtor was always liable. This implies, that *mora debitoris* transferred the risk of supervening impossibility from the creditor onto the debtor.

This rule applied to all obligations.

With regard to *negotia fonae fidei, mora debitoris* had another consequence, namely that the debtor did not only have to pay a sum of money equal to the value of the performance but had to pay all damages suffered by the creditor as a result of the *mora*.

Mora debitoris could be extinguished by an offer to perform even if the creditor refused to accept the performance.

This brings us to a second aspect of *mora* namely *mora creditoris*, when a creditor refused *sine iusta causa*, without good reason, the tender of performance by the debtor.

Firstly the performance tendered has to be the due performance and this is a question of fact.

Secondly an actual tender of performance was required.

The consequences of *mora creditoris* were that the debtor is thereafter liable only for *dolus*, i.e. only in cases where he intentionally made performance impossible. In all other cases the risk was the creditor's.

Furthermore, the debtor became entitled to reimbursement for damages suffered as a result of mora creditoris. He had a lien which he exercised by way of the *exceptio doli*. Finally *more creditoris* extinguished *mora debitoris*.

11. Defects in agreement

It has been seen, that in later law, *contractus* signified a legal act based on the *consensus* by the parties to create an obligation.

The fact that the concept of a contract gradually changed, was a consequence of the progress of Roman law.

The strictly formal legal acts of the old *ius civile* disappeared or were adapted while new legal acts of the *ius gentium* were assimilated into Roman law. These legal acts were informal and the intention of the parties was the deciding factor.

By the time agreement became a requirement for a valid contract no contract was concluded if the agreement was defective, even if the other requirement (i.e. *re, verbis* or *litteris*) was fulfilled.

The main forms whereby the agreement might be affected are *error*, mistake, *dolus*, fraud and *metus*, duress.

12. Error

Error is present when one or both parties labour, under a *bona fide* mistake. At the conclusion of a contract the mistake had to be made *bona fide*, in good faith, and must not be induced by fraud. A mistake is a wrong impression of the actual facts.

Originally, *error* was only relevant with regard to the *contractus consensu*, next with regard to all contracts based on good faith and finally, even with regard to contracts *stricti iuris.*

However, there are various types of *error* and different consequences must be catelogued:

Error in negotio, mistake as to the nature of the legal act which is entered into. No valid transaction was concluded.

Error in corpore, mistake regarding the object of the contract, viz. performance. No valid contract was concluded.

Error in nomine, mistake regarding the name of the object of the contract, but both parties had the same object in mind. This type of mistake was irrelevant and a valid contract was concluded.

Error in persona, mistake regarding the identity of the other contracting party. Only if the contract was entered into with regard to a certain person was this form of mistake relevant.

Error in substantia, error as to the nature or quality of the object of the contract.

In this case, there is agreement about the object of the contract but one or both parties were mistaken about an essential quality of the object.

In classical law, this type of mistake was irrelevant but in later law the contract was void if the *error* was made about the essence of the object. This philosophical approach, (what is the essence of an object?) has little practical value.

Error as to the motive for the formation of a contract was in principle irrelevant but can in some cases by construed as *error in substantia.*

13. Dolus

Dolus, fraud, consisted of any guile, chicanery or trick used to circumvent, defraud or dupe another person.

According to the old *ius civile* the fact that a person was induced to conclude a contract by fraud was irrelevant, in other words the contract was perfectly valid.

Towards the end of the republican era the *praetor* brought about a change by granting the *exceptio doli* to a party who was induced to conclude a contract from the *ius civile* by means of fraud.

This implies that the contract in question was not *ipso iure*, automatically, void, but the victim of the fraud could raise the *exceptio doli* as a defence against the action arising from the contract.

It should be noted that *stipulatio*, the most important and typical contract of Roman law was derived from the *ius civile.*

If the contract entered into in consequence of fraud was based on *bona fides* the *exceptio doli* would be superfluous; in that instance the parties were required to perform in accordance with good faith and good faith did not require performance of an obligation resulting from a contract concluded as a result of fraud.

However, the contract was not void because the victim of the fraud could institute a claim for damages based on the contract against the perpetrator.

The *exceptio doli* had a second application, which may be seen in the formula *si in ea re nihil dolo malo Auli Agerii factum sit neque fiat*, if in this affair nothing has been done or is done fraudulently by Aulus Agerius, i.e. the plaintiff.

This illustrates that a claim could be defeated, if the plaintiff had committed fraud against the defendant in the past, i.e. at the moment the contract was entered into, or in the present, i.e. at the moment of enforcing an action.

As the scope of the *exceptio doli* was so wide, a distinction can be made between the *exceptio doli specialis* or *praeteriti*, the defence against fraud committed at the moment of contracting and the *exceptio doli generalis* or *praesentis*, the defence against fraud at the time of *litis contestatio*, i.e. the moment of instituting the action.

14. Metus

Metus, duress, consisted in the use of force or the threat of force as a result of which a reasonable person would fear danger to his person, property or his family.

According to the old *ius civile* it was irrelevant whether a person was induced by duress to conclude a contract; in other words, the contract was perfectly valid. Earlier, in the case of fraud the *praetor* came to the aid of the defendant by granting the *exceptio metus causa* where he (the defendant) was forced into the conclusion of a contract from the *ius civile* by means of duress. This implies that the contract in question was not *ipso iure*, automatically, void, but that the person who had suffered duress could raise the *exceptio metus causa* as a defence against the action arising from the contract.

If the contract entered into in consequence of duress was based on *bona fides*, the *exceptio metus causa* was superfluos; in that case the parties were required to perform in accordance with good faith and good faith did not require performance of an obligation resulting from a contract concluded as a result of duress. However, the contract was not void as the victim of duress could institute a claim for damages based on the contract against the perpetrator.

15. Condition

Condicio, a condition, is an uncertain future event.

A condition may be attached to virtually any legal act and thus also to a contract. The effect of the legal act is then made dependant on the realization or not of a future uncertain event.

A distinction must be made between suspensive and resolutive conditions.

A suspensive condition is one which suspends the effect of the legal act until the condition is realized. It follows that when a suspensive condition is contained in a contract an obligation only arises if the condition is fulfilled. Until this happens there is no obligation but merely a *spes,* a hope, and if the condition is never fulfilled no obligation will ever arise.

A resolutive condition is one which discharges the effect of a legal act the moment the condition is fulfilled. Prior to the fulfilment of the condition the legal act has full effect. It follows that when a resolutive condition is attached to a contract an obligation is created immediately but the moment the condition is fulfilled the existing obligation is terminated.

Several types of conditions can be distinguished:

Positive and negative conditions

A condition is positive when its fulfilment depends upon the happening of a future uncertain event. It is negative when it depends upon the future uncertain event not happening.

Condicio potestativa and condicio casualis

A *condicio potestativa* is a potestative condition where the fulfilment is in the control of the one or the other of the parties. A *condicio casualis* is a casual condition where the realization is dependent upon chance and not within the control of the parties.

An impossible condition attached to a contract caused the whole contract to be null and void as was the case of conditions tainted by illegality and immorality.

A condition is a future uncertain event. When the effect of a legal act is made subject to the happening or not happening of an event in the past or present, the actual situation must be assessed and the legal act is valid or void depending on this situation.

Originally, resolutive conditions were ineffective in respect of *negotia stricti iuris*. These legal acts were entered into formally and could only be terminated in a formal way.

However, the *praetor* gave effect to such conditions by means of the *exceptio pacti conventi* or the *exceptio doli.*

In the case of negotia *bonae fidei* this problem did not exist since the *negotia* could be entered into informally and could, therefore, be terminated in an informal way.

16. Term

Dies, a term, is a future certain event. A term may be attached to virtually any legal act and this also to a contract.

The effect of the legal act is then made dependant on the happening of a future certain event.

A distinction must be drawn between suspensive and resolutive terms.

A suspensive term is one which suspends the legal effect of a legal act until the term is completed. It therefore follows, that when a suspensive term is embodied in a contract, an obligation arises immediately, but its performance can be claimed and enforced only at the time of completion of the term.

A resolutive term is one which terminates the effect of legal act the moment the term is completed. Thus, when a resolutive term is incorporated into a contract an obligation is created immediately, but the moment the term is completed, the existing obligation is discharged.

A further distinction can be made between *dies certus* and *dies incertus.*

In either case the future event is one which is bound to occur, but in the case of *dies incertus* it is uncertain as to exactly when that day is going to come.

Originally, resolutive terms were ineffective in respect of *negotia stricti iuris.* However, the *praetor* gave effect to such terms by means of the *exceptio pacti conventi* or the *exceptio doli.*

17. Modus

Modus, a charge, is where a beneficiary is charged to do something.

A charge could only be added to certain legal acts, these were mainly donations, *manumissiones* or bequests.

A *modus* was usually added for sacral or social purposes.

The beneficiary acquired the benefit immediately, thus the acquisition of the benefit was not dependant on the execution of the charge. Moreover, a *modus* was not enforceable in classical law. In later law an interested party could enforce the charge and in cases where there was no interested party the state or church could enforce it. Justinian introduced the possibility of recovering the benefit if the beneficiary did not execute the charge.

18. Representation

We deal with representation when a representative enters into a legal act which has legal effect for his principal.

The principle which applied in Roman law was that a legal act was a personal affair which could only have legal effect with regard to the parties participating in the legal act. In other words, Roman law did not recognize representation. This principle applied to all legal acts for example transfer of ownership, litigation, contracting etc. Maxims used to denote the principle were *per extraneam personam nobis adquiri non potest*, you cannot acquire (ownership, possession, real rights or personal rights) by way of an agent, and *alteri stipulari nemo potest*, nobody can enter into a contract by means of a representative. This principle did not apply only to the *stipulatio*-contract but to all contracts. Since such a principle curtails legal development and is practically undesirable, exceptions were gradually recognized.

A distinction must be made between acquisitive representation and agency imposing liability on the principal.

In the first case the agent acquires something, such as ownership, possession, a real or personal right for his principal, while in the second case the agent binds his principal by his legal act.

It was especially with regard to acquisitive representation that many exceptions were recognized:

Within the sphere of the *familia* the persons *in potestate*, under the power of the *paterfamilias* (the family superior), in other words his slaves and *alieni iuris* persons could acquire anything which then vested automatically in the *dominus*, master, or *paterfamilias.*

A *cognitor* or *procurator* who originally acted as a representative in litigation was in later law appointed to manage somebody's affairs. In classical law ownership and possession could be acquired by the *cognitor* or *procurator* for his principal. In the law of Justinian a *procurator* could acquire any rights for his principal.

A *tutor* and *curator* could in classical law acquire ownership and possession for persons under tutelage or curatorship; in the law of Justinian these persons could acquire any rights for the *pupillus* or ward.

With regard to agency imposing liability on the principal, Roman law recognized few exceptions. The most important exceptions are found within the *familia*, where the *praetor* introduced the so-called *actiones adiecticiae qualitatis*.

19. Actiones adiecticiae qualitatis

Actiones adiecticiae qualitatis were actions by which a third party who had entered into a legal act with a slave or *filiusfamilias,* a son in *potestate*, could sue the master or *paterfamilias.* It can be said, that in certain cases, agency which imposed liability on the principal by a slave or *filiusfamilias* was recognized.

Actio quod iussu

Where the *paterfamilias* or *dominus* had given a *iussum*, authorization or instruction, to a third party to enter into transactions with his son or slave, the father or master was liable *in solidum*, in full, with the *actio quod iussu*, for obligations undertaken within the limits of the authorization.

Actio exercitoria

Where a father or master appointed his son or slave as master of a ship, he could be held liable in full with the *actio exercitoria* for obligations incurred by the son or slave in connexion with his activities as master of the ship. This action was even applicable where an independant free person was appointed as master of a ship.

Actio institutoria

Where a slave, son or independent free person was appointed as manager of a business, third parties could institute this action against the *pater* or master for all the liabilities incurred by the slave, son or independant free person within the scope of the business.

Actio de peculio

In practice the *filiusfamilias* and able slaves were given a *peculium*, property in the form of money or goods, to use and to trade with.

The *peculium* was and remained the property of the father or master.

The father or master could be held liable by third parties with the *actio de peculio*, for obligations entered into by the son or slave, with regard to the *peculium*.

His liability was, however, limited to the extent of the *peculium* as at the time of judgment. The father or master was not liable *in solidum*, but here we find the principle of limited liability.

Actio de in rem verso

Where a slave or son had entered into transactions by which the estate of the master or father had benefitted, third parties could sue the master or father with this action for the amount by which he had been enriched.

The *actio de in rem verso* was, therefore, an enrichment action.

A combination of the last two actions was also possible.

20. A contract in favour of a third party

Since Roman law did not recognize, in principle, representation in legal acts, a contract conferring benefits or imposing duties upon third parties had no effect. A contract was considered a personal affair which only created an obligation between the contracting parties.

This principle was stringly adhered to with regard to contracts by which performance was to be undertaken by a third party; i.e. a contract imposing duties on a third party was void. On the other hand, with regard to acquisitive representation, i.e. a contract entered into in favour of a third party, exceptions to the general rule were gradually admitted:

The slave and the *filiusfamilias* could contract in favour of their master or father.

In exceptional cases an *actio utilis* or *actio in factum* was granted to a third party to enforce a provision made in his favour.

When it was stipulated that performance should be undertaken in favour of the contracting party and a third party; only the contracting party acquired a personal right, for half the performance only.

When performance was stipulated in favour of the contracting party or a third party; only the contracting party acquired a personal right for the full performance. The third party acquired no right, but the debtor had the option to perform in favour of the contracting party or in favour of the third party. The third party was *solutionis causa adiectus*, added for purposes of performance.

Justinian refers to the solution developed in legal practice, namely the making of a penal stipulation. One stipulated a penalty payable to oneself while performance in favour of a third party was entered as a condition in the contract.

For example *Centum mihi dari, si Stichum servum Titio non dederis spondesne?*, Do you promise to pay me one hundred, if you do not give the slave *Stichus to Titius*. The third party did not acquire a right but the pressure of the penalty will ensure performance to the third party.

Justinian also validated stipulations in favour of an heir.

21. Plurality of debtors and/or creditors

It can happen that there are more creditors or more debtors as well as a plurality of creditors and debtors for one obligation.

Regarding obligations arising from contract or *quasi*-contract the divisibility of the performance was of importance.

If performance was divisible, i.e. could be completed in instalments without changing its character, the obligation was divided into as many obligations as there were debtors and/or creditors. Each debtor was liable for his *pro rata*, proportionate, share of the performance; while each creditor was entitled to his *pro rata* share of the performance.

Should the performance be indivisible there was only one obligation.

Each debtor was liable for the full performance and each creditor was entitled to the whole of that which was due.

However, if one debtor performed the whole of what was due, the obligation was terminated, in other words the other debtors are discharged and the other creditors have no further claim. The debtor who had performed had a right of recourse against his fellow-debtors and the creditor who received the performance had a duty to share with his fellow-creditors. However, this possibility depended upon the legal relationship which existed between the parties.

An obligation could also be discharged in ways other than performance. The effect of *litiscontestatio* played an important part. In classical law *litiscontestatio* extinguished the obligation. Justinian abolished this rule and decreed that only full satisfaction of the obligation discharged the obligation.

Where every debtor is liable *in solidum* and every creditor entitled *in solidum* the obligation is described as solidary. This is the case where performance is indivisible or where parties stipulated as such.

22. Contractus re

Contractus re were contracts which were constituted by agreement and delivery.

Delivery is transfer of possession, physical control of a tangible thing.

It is dependant on the *causa*, reason, for the transfer of possession, whether ownership or possession (protected or not) passes from the transferor to the transferee.

Once delivery had taken place the *contractus re* was operative. As soon as the contract was constituted one or more obligations arose.

In the case of *contractus re* the principle obligation was always to return the same thing or the equivalent.

23. Mutuum

Mutuum, loan for consumption, was the oldest *contractus re* which originated from the old *ius civile* and was therefore a *negotium stricti iuris.*

Mutuum was constituted by agreement and the transfer of a thing.

The parties agreed that the one party would lend a specific object to the other for consumption and that the second party would at a later stage return an object of the same kind, quality and quantity.

By means of delivery ownership passed to the borrower since he had to have the right to consume the thing.

The thing in question is therefore a *res consumptibilis*, a thing which is consumed by use, as well as a *res fungibilis*, a thing that can be replaced by an equivalent. *Res fungibiles* are also generic things, things specified according to type, of which the most important example is money.

Mutuum is a unilateral contract; only one obligation is created. The lender has a personal right (he is creditor) against the borrower, while a duty is imposed on the borrower.

The duty of the borrower (i.e. the right of the lender) is to restore an equivalent amount of the same kind and quality to the lender. The creditor could enforce his personal right with a personal action, the *condictio;* where a loan of money was involved the *condictio certae creditae pecuniae;* where the loan applied to wheat the *condictio triticaria;* and in all other cases the *condictio certae rei* was available.

The *condictio* was a personal action by which the plaintiff claimed a *certum*, a specific object or specific amount of money or specific amount of generic things. This action derived from the *ius civile* and was therefore an *actio civilis*. This entailed that with the *condictio* the precise amount or quantity had to be claimed and in cases where more or less was claimed the action floundered. It was, therefore, necessary to demand interest by way of another contract, namely the *stipulatio* and to claim the interest with a separate action. If interest had been agreed upon informally this agreement was unenforceable.

With regard to *negotia stricti iuris* the *exceptiones (doli, metus causa, pacti conventi)* were relevant.

CONTRACTUAL LIABILITY AND RISK

As ownership passed to the borrower no question arose concerning contractual liability. Moreover, performance could never become impossible, since *genera non pereunt.*

SENATUS CONSULTUM MACEDONIANUM

This *senatus consultum* forbade loans of money to a *filiusfamilias.*

However, the enactment did not provide that such *mutuum* would be *ipso iure*, automatically, void, but gave the *exceptio senatus consulti Macedoniani* against the action of the lender. The loan could, therefore, not be enforced and a *naturalis obligatio* existed.

24. Commodatum

Commodatum, loan for use, originated from the *ius honorarium* and was therefore a *negotium bonae fidei.*

Commodatum was constituted by agreement and the transfer of a thing.

The parties agreed that the one party would lend a certain object to the other for use and that the second party would at a later stage return the same thing.

By delivery only, detention passes to the borrower; ownership and protected possession remained with the *commodans* or *commodator*, the lender.

The thing in question is, therefore, a *res non consumptibilis*, a thing that is not consumed by use, as well as a *res non fungibilis*, a thing that can not be replaced by an equivalent, since there is question of a specific thing.

Commodatum has to be gratuitous; if there is remuneration the contract would be one of *locatio et conductio*, letting and hiring).

Commodatum is an imperfectly bilateral contract, i.e. in principle, the contract gives rise to one obligation only. However, it is possible for a counterclaim to arise.

The main obligation which always arises is the duty of the *commodatarius*, the borrower, to return the same thing to the lender after use or at a definite date.

The creditor (i.e. *commodator*, lender) could enforce his personal right with a personal action, namely, the *actio commodati.*

However, the possibility exists that the borrower has a counterclaim, namely, if he suffered damages as a result of the *dolus* of the lender or if he incurred exceptional expense in looking after the thing. He could then institute the *actio commodati contraria* against the *commodator.*

Both actions derived from the *ius honorarium* and were, therefore, based on the *bona fides.* This implies that the duties of both parties were defined by the requirements of good faith.

CONTRACTUAL LIABILITY AND RISK

In classical law the *commodatarius* was held liable for *custodia*. Hence he would only be not answerable if impossibility of performance, the failure to return the thing, was attributable to *vis major*. In other words if the thing was damaged or destroyed by *vis major*, the *commodator* (in most cases also the owner of the thing) carried the risk. If the thing in question was damaged or destroyed as a result of *dolus, culpa* or *casus fortuitus* of the borrower he was liable, i.e. the *commodator* could institute the *actio commodati* against him for damages.

The reason for this strict degree of liability is found in the fact that *commodatum* is gratuitous and that the borrower profits from the contract. In the law of Justinian the *commodatarius* was liable for *culpa levis in abstracto*. Consequently the *commodator* carried the risk for *vis major* and *casus fortuitus*.

25. Depositum

Depositum, deposit originated from the *ius honorarium* and was therefore a *negotium bonae fidei*.

Depositum was constituted by agreement and the transfer of a thing.

The parties agreed that the one party would hand over a movable thing to the other and that the second party would gratuitously keep the thing for him and would return it to the former at his wish.

The delivery causes only detention to pass to the depositary; ownership and protected possession remain with the *depositor*.

The thing in question must be a movable.

Depositum must be gratuitous; if there was any remuneration the contract would be one of *locatio et conductio*, letting and hiring. The depositary was not entitled to use the property; to do so constituted *furtum*.

Depositum is an imperfectly bilateral contract, i.e. the contract in principle gives rise to one obligation only. However, it is possible for a counterclaim to arise. The main obligation is always the duty of the *depositarius*, depositary, to return the thing on demand to the depositor. The creditor (i.e. depositor) could enforce his personal right with a personal action, the *actio depositi*.

However, the possibility exists that the depositary has a counterclaim, namely, if he had suffered damages as a result of the *dolus* of the depositor or if he had incurred expense.

In that event he could then institute the *actio depositi contraria* against the depositor.

Both actions derived from the *ius honorarium* and were therefore based on the *bona fides*. This implies that the duties of both parties were defined by the requirements of good faith.

CONTRACTUAL LIABILITY AND RISK

The depositary was held liable only for *dolus* and *culpa lata*. Hence, he would not be answerable if impossibility of performance, the failure to return the thing, was attributable to *vis major, casus fortuitus* and all *culpa* except *culpa lata*. In other words, if the thing was damaged or destroyed the depositor (in most cases also the owner of the thing) carried the risk for everything except *dolus* and *culpa lata*. Only in those two extremes could the depositor institute the *actio depositi* against the depositary for damages.

The reason for this light degree of liability is the fact that *depositum* is gratuitous and in the interest of the depositor. However, condemnation on grounds of the *actio depositi* involved *infamia*, infamy.

Three special cases of deposit can be distinguished:

Depositum necessarium or *miserabile*, deposit made out of necessity. The duty and liability of the depositary were the same as regards normal deposit. If he was found to be liable, however, he was condemned *in duplum*, double.

Deposit of a thing over which a dispute existed to the care of a *sequester*. The *sequester* acquired protected possession. The action bore the special name *actio depositi sequestraria*.

DEPOSITUM IRREGULARE

Deposit of money or other consumptibles, on the terms that the depositary may consume this and, at a later stage, will return the equivalent.

The most important example is money deposited with a banker.

Since consumptibles are involved ownership passes to the depositary.

Originally, this contractual relationship was considered to be *mutuum*, but gradually *depositum irregulare* became a separate entity. This transaction is primarily in the interest of the depositor, while *mutuum* is in the interest of the borrower. Moreover, there was the advantage that the *actio depositi* was based on the *bona fides* and interest which had been agreed upon informally could be claimed by this action.

26. Pignus

Pignus, pledge which originated from the *ius honorarium* and was therefore a *negotium bonae fidei*.

Pignus was constituted by agreement and the transfer of a thing.

The parties agreed that the one party would hand over a thing as security for a debt and that the other party would return the property if the debt was duly paid.

By the delivery *possessio ad interdicta* (a form of protected possession) passed to the pledgee; ownership remained with the pledgor.

The thing in question had to be tangible.

The pledgee was, in principle, not allowed to use the pledged object or sell it; this would constitute *furtum*, theft. However, *antichresis* (an agreement by which the pledgee could use the object) and the *pactum distrahendi* (an agreement by which the pledgee could sell the object) were frequently entered into and the *pactum distrahendi* became a *ius distrahendi*, a right to alienate the object.

Pignus is an imperfectly bilateral contract; i.e. the contract, in principle, gives rise to one obligation only. However, the possibility of a counterclaim exists. The main obligation which always arises, is the duty of the pledgee to return the pledged object if the debt is duly paid.

The creditor of this obligation, i.e. the pledgor, could enforce his personal right with a personal action, the *actio pigneraticia.*

However, the possibility exists that the pledgee has a counterclaim, namely, if he had suffered damages as the result of the *dolus* of the pledgor or if he had incurred expenses. He could then institute the *actio pigneraticia contraria* against the pledgor.

Both actions derived from the *ius honorarium* and were therefore based on the *bona fides.* This implies that the duties of both parties were defined by the requirements of good faith.

When the *ius distrahendi* had become a reality and the pledgee was entitled to sell the pledged object if the secured debt was not satisfied, the pledgor could claim the *superfluum*, the excess funds, with the *actio pigneraticia.*

CONTRACTUAL LIABILITY AND RISK

In classical law the pledgee was held liable for *custodia.* Hence, he would not be answerable only where the impossibility of performance, the failure to return the pledged thing, was attributable to *vis major.*

If the pledged thing was damaged or destroyed by *vis major*, the pledgor (in most cases also the owner of the thing) carried the risk.

If the thing in question was damaged as a result of *dolus, culpa* or *casus fortuitus* by the pledgee he was liable, in other words, the pledgor could institute the *actio pigneraticia* against him for damages.

In the law of Justinian the pledgee was liable for *culpa levis in abstracto*. The pledgor consequently carried the risk for *vis major* and *casus fortuitus.*

27. Contractus verbis

Contractus verbis were contracts which were constituted by agreement and *verbis solemnibus*, formal words. One of the earliest known contracts is *sponsio*, a *contractus verbis* with religious elements. *Sponsio* was superseded by the *stipulatio*, the most important and typical contract of Roman law. Both *sponsio* and *stipulatio* were typical of the *ius civile* and therefore *negotia stricti iuris*. The result of this was that, originally, only the formalities were of importance and the question whether *consensus*, agreement had been reached between the parties was irrelevant. In late classical law *consensus* became an essential requirement of the *contractus verbis*.

28. Stipulatio

Stipulatio was constituted by agreement and formal words.

The element of agreement acquired legal importance only in classical law.

With regard to *negotia stricti iuris* the *exceptiones (doli, metus causa, pacti conventi)* were relevant.

The *verbis solemnibus* requirement consisted in the formalities of question and answer and the same verb had to be used in the question and the answer. The answer had to follow the question immediately which implies that a *stipulatio* could only be concluded *inter praesentes*, where the parties are in each other's presence.

It should be noted this was the most important drawback of the *stipulatio*, because practical considerations require contracts which can be concluded *inter absentes*, where the parties are not in each other's presence.

Originally the verb *spondere* had to be used in question and answer, but gradually other verbs of promise could be used: *promittere, dare, facere, fideiubere*, the Greek equivalents of the Latin words of promise, but question and answer had to correspond.

In 472 A.D. the Emperor Leo enacted a *constitutio* which abrogated the *verbis solemnibus* requirement; agreement expressed in any words was all that was required.

Stipulatio, however, remained a *contractus verbis*, after 472, because words were still necessary. Also it continued to be necessary that the parties be in each other's presence.

Stipulatio was the most important contract of Roman law, because any lawful performance could be made binding. In other words the application of the *stipulatio* was without limit. Moreover, the performance was precisely defined in the question.

Finally, the *stipulatio* was formal, but the formalities were not time-consuming or difficult. As a result of the formalities, there was no doubt as to the precise moment at which the obligation arose, namely when the debtor answered *spondeo*.

For purposes of evidence, a *stipulatio* was generally recorded in writing. A document was drawn up to prove that a *stipulatio* was concluded. The obligation arose, however, from the words since *stipulatio* always remained a verbal contract. A verbal contract recorded in writing was known as a *cautio*.

For purposes of evidence, witnesses could also be used.

The presence of witnesses, or the recording in writing were never requirements for the validity of the *stipulatio*. If no witnesses were present or *cautio* drawn up, the *stipulatio* was valid, but the furnishing of evidence could create problems.

Stipulatio was a unilateral contract; i.e. only one obligation was created. The *stipulator* (the creditor, the party who asked the question) had a personal right against the *promissor* (the debtor, the party who answered *spondeo* or *promitto* or *dabo* etc.).

The duty of the *promissor*, i.e. the right of the *stipulator*, was performance in favour of the creditor of exactly what had been stipulated in the question.

The creditor could enforce his personal right with a personal action, the *condictio* where performance was *certum*, specific; where performance was *incertum*, non specific, the *actio ex stipulatu* was used.

CONTRACTUAL LIABILITY AND RISK

When performance became impossible after the conclusion of the contract, the debtor was in principle discharged from liability. Gradually a clause by which the debtor undertook that peformance would not become impossible on his account was implied: *factum debitoris perpetuat obligationem*, a positive act on the part of the debtor perpetuates the obligation and *mora debitoris perpetuat obligationem, mora* on the part of the debtor perpetuates the obligation. This meant, that in case of supervening impossibility of performance the *promissor*, debtor, was released from liability except where *factum* or *mora debitoris* applied. Therefore, in principle the creditor carried the risk, but in case of *factum* or *mora debitoris* he could institute an action against the debtor for the pecuniary value of the impossible performance.

29. Contractus litteris

Contractus litteris were contracts which were constituted by agreement and formal writing.

These contracts did not play an important role in Roman law, since the legal acts of Roman law were in principle constituted orally and writing only constituted evidence.

30. Contractus consensu

Contractus consensu were contracts which were constituted by agreement.

Agreement, however manifested, was sufficient to create the four *contractus consensu*. They all had their origin in the *ius gentium* and were, therefore, *negotia bonae fidei*, which means that the duties of the parties were defined by the requirements of good faith.

31. Emptio et venditio

Emptio et venditio, purchase and sale together with *stipulatio* formed the most common and most important of contracts.

A contract of sale was concluded as soon as the parties had reached agreement regarding three *essentialia*, viz to buy and to sell, the *merx*, the object of the sale and the *pretium*, the price.

No formalities were required with regard to the agreement which could be reached in any way, viz by way of words, letters, messenger, signs, behaviour in a certain manner etc.

The parties did not have to be in each other's presence and all consensual contracts could be concluded *inter absentes.*

The giving of *arra*, earnest, was not a requisite for the conclusion of the Roman contract of sale. However, the parties could agree that *arra* would be given for evidentiary purposes. In later law a right to withdraw or forfeit the *arra* appears to have developed.

It also became practice to record a Roman sale in writing as a probative instrument. Finally, if the parties agreed to reduce the contract of sale to writing, the contract was only concluded the moment at which that had been done; unless and until the document had been drawn up, there would be no contract.

Firstly, the parties had to agree that one person wished to buy and another wished to sell. On this point *error in negotio* could arise.

MERX

Secondly, the parties had to agree on the object of the sale. The object had to be *certum*, specific. The contract of sale was concluded only when it was certain *quid, quale, quantum emptum sit*, what, which quality and how much is bought. Consequently, the consensual contract of sale was only possible with regard to a specific thing or specific things in Roman law and sales of *genera*, i.e. sales of objects described by *genus* or kind, for example ten bags of wheat, were not recognized by Roman law. Things of a kind, *genera*, were 'purchased and sold' by way of two *stipulationes.*

The object sold had to be *in commercio.*

There was no requirement that the object sold had to be the property of the vendor, i.e. it was possible to sell another's property. Only where a person bought his own property was the contract of sale void.

The object sold had to be still in existence at the time of contracting: *impossibilium nulla obligatio est.* If, however, the vendor knew that the thing had ceased to exist, he acted contrary to the *bona fides* and could be sued for damages with the *actio empti.*

The thing need not already be in existence at the time of conclusion of the contract, in other words *res futurae*, future things, could be sold.

A distinction must be drawn between *emptio spei*, the purchase of an expectancy, and *emptio rei speratae*, the purchase of an object expected to come into being.

Emptio spei, is an unconditional sale of an expectancy for a specific price. Even if nothing materializes, the sale is good.

Emptio rei speratae, is a conditional sale. If the thing materializes, there is a contract, if nothing materializes, there is no contract.

PRETIUM

Thirdly, the parties had to agree on the *pretium*, the price.

The price must be in money. Otherwise the transaction would be *permutatio rerum*, barter. The agreement to barter was a *nudum pactum* and became actionable only in post-classical law. Moreover, the distinction between sale and barter is important since the duties of the buyer and the seller are different and consequently the buyer has to be distinguished from the seller.

The price had to be *certum*, fixed. In classical law, there was a difference of opinion whether the price could be fixed by a third party or not.

Justinian recognized the validity of this type of sale and ruled it to be a conditional sale; if the third party did not want to, or could not fix the price, no contract of sale came into effect.

The price had to be *verum* or *iustum*, i.e. the price had more or less, to correspond to the value of the *merx*.

In classical law, the parties enjoyed complete freedom regarding the fixing of the price. Even where the price was unrealistic, the contract was valid, unless there was a question of *dolus*, in which case the aggrieved party had an action. In post-classical law, the so-called *laesio enormis* rule, i.e. serious loss rule, developed: if the price was less than half the value of the object it was possible to rescind the sale.

The seller could claim back the object and return the price. The buyer could prevent rescission by making up the price to the full value. Roman law did not, however, provide an analogous remedy for the buyer who had paid an unrealistically high price.

Emptio et venditio is a synallagmatic contract, i.e. two obligations arise; both parties to the contract of sale have a personal right against the other party; both parties have a duty against the other party. The contract is aimed at an exchange of performances.

This contract developed from the *ius gentium* and was therefore, based on the *bona fides*. Consequently, the duties of both parties were defined by the requirements of good faith.

32. Duties of the buyer

Firstly, the buyer had to pay the price to the seller. In principle this had to be done on the day of delivery of the object sold, however, the parties could agree on another time.

Depending on special circumstances the buyer could have further duties, for example in the case of *mora debitoris* on his part he would be liable for interest.

Furthermore, it could happen that the seller incurred expenses necessary to maintain the object during the period between the contracting of the sale and delivery. In such a case the buyer would have to reimburse the seller for such expenses.

Finally, the buyer could lapse into *mora creditoris* and would be liable for expenses incurred in the upkeep of the object sold.

DID THE BUYER HAVE TO PAY THE PRICE EVEN IF THE OBJECT WAS NOT DELIVERED TO HIM?

For the answer to this question a distinction must be drawn between the case where the seller did not want to perform and the case where the seller could not perform as a result of loss or damage suffered by the object, after the contract of sale.

In the first instance, the buyer did not have to pay the agreed price. Both parties to a contract of sale were under the obligation of *dare facere ex fide bona* and the *bona fides* did not require that the buyer had to pay where the seller did not want to deliver.

The second possibility is more complicated and an answer was found in accordance with the contractual liability of the vendor and the rule *periculum est emptoris*, the risk is borne by the buyer. This means that if performance, i.e. delivery of the thing sold, became impossible as a result of a fact which fell within the liability of the seller, the buyer was not bound to pay the price, but could, with the *actio empti*, sue the seller for damages.

However, if performance became impossible as the result of *casus fortuitus* or *vis major*, (which fell outside the seller's liability), the seller was freed from his duty to perform, but the buyer still had to pay the price. This is worded in the maxim *'Periculum est emptoris'* the risk is with the buyer.

The duties of the buyer are the rights of the seller. The seller could enforce his personal rights with a personal action, the *actio venditi*.

33. Duties of the seller

VACUAM POSSESSIONEM TRADERE

The first duty of the seller was *vacuam possessionem tradere*, he had to give free and undisturbed possession of the thing sold to the purchaser. The seller must deliver the thing sold in accordance with the contract description, together with all accessions to it, or fruits of it, which had arisen between the conclusion of the contract and delivery.

In cases where the seller delivered less than this, the buyer could sue him, with the *actio empti*, for the monetary value, even in cases where the seller had been *bona fide*.

It may be noted that the vendor was not bound to transfer the ownership of the thing sold to the purchaser. In this context the following possibilities occurred.

Firstly, where the seller was the owner of the thing sold, the contract of sale was a *iusta causa traditionis* and in classical Roman law, delivery of the *merx* transferred ownership upon the buyer.

Justinian decreed that the ownership of the thing sold did not pass to the purchaser despite delivery to him, unless the full purchase price was paid, credit had been granted or security had been provided. (This should be compared with the law of things *supra*.)

The second possibility was that the seller was not the owner of the *merx*. In this case the *nemo plus iuris* rule applied, with the result that the buyer did not receive ownership, but the possibility of *usucapio* remained open. Finally, the seller could have fraudulently sold and delivered somebody else's thing. In the last two cases the possibility existed that the owner might appear and institute the *reivindicatio* to assert his ownership. Only in the case where the seller had acted fraudulently could the buyer institute the *actio empti* for damages. In the other cases the buyer had to carry the loss. Consequently, a further duty on the vendor developed in time.

GUARANTEE AGAINST EVICTION

Eviction takes place where the buyer loses possession of the object sold, as the result of the instituting of an *actio in rem*; for example *reivindicatio, actio Publiciana, actio Serviana, vindicatio ususfructus*. Successful institution of a *vindicatio servitutis* did not amount to eviction, since the defendant would not lose his possession, but in such a case the buyer was not given *vacua possessio*.

Originally when the formal *mancipatio* cash sale was in use, the buyer who was evicted could institute the *actio auctoritatis* for twice the price against the vendor.

However, *mancipatio* was not always a possibility, viz in cases where *res nec mancipi* were sold or where *peregrini* were involved. Quite early on it became the practice in such cases to enter into *stipulationes*, in which the vendor undertook to reimburse the buyer in the event of his being evicted. These *stipulationes* were, therefore, subject ot a suspensive condition.

The various *stipulationes* used in this context were the *stipulatio duplae (pecuniae)* where the vendor promised to pay double the price to the buyer if he should be evicted; the *stipulatio simplae* and the *stipulatio habere licere* where reimbursement of the damage suffered by the buyer as a result of *evictio* was promised by the seller.

Nevertheless, if there were no *mancipatio* or no *stipulatio*, the buyer carried the loss of eviction, unless he could prove fraud on the part of the vendor, in which case he had the *actio empti* at his disposal.

During the classical period a further development took place, by reason of the *bonae fidei* nature of the contract of sale. The first step was that the *bona fides* required the vendor to enter into one of the stipulations while finally, the *bona fides* required that in all cases of eviction the buyer could hold the seller liable for damages with the *actio empti.* This means that a stipulation was no longer necessary because an implicit guarantee against eviction existed. The buyer could enforce this guarantee with the *actio empti.* With this action he claimed for damages, in other words the pecuniary value of the loss suffered as a result of the eviction. This can be much more than just the price, since *lucrum cessans*, the profit the buyer had to forgo, and *damnum emergens*, consequential loss, were included.

CONTRACTUAL LIABILITY AND RISK

Because sale was a *bonae fidei* contract the vendor had, during conclusion of the contract, to act in good faith.

In Justinian law this meant that the seller was liable for *dolus* and *culpa levis in abstracto.* In other words, if the purchaser was to suffer damages through fraud or negligence on the part of the vendor, the purchaser could institute the *actio empti* and hold the seller liable for these damages. Once the contract was concluded, the vendor remained liable for *dolus* and *culpa levis in abstracto*, in respect of the thing sold until delivery.

CARE OF THING SOLD

This brings us to another duty of the seller, i.e. care of the thing sold until delivery. It was not necessary that the object sold was delivered immediately the contract of sale was *perfecta*, but a considerable period of time might elapse between the contracting of the sale and the delivery. During this period, the object sold could be destroyed, damaged or lost and the vendor was liable for *dolus* and *culpa levis in abstracto;* in short he had a duty to take care of the object sold, as a *bonus paterfamilias.* The effect of this was that, if the object sold had been destroyed or damaged in the period between the making of the contract sale and the delivery as a result of wilful or negligent activity on the part of the vendor, he is liable for damages; thus the buyer could institute the *actio empti* against him to claim for damages. If the object sold is not delivered to the buyer as the result of a fact within the liability of the seller, the buyer does not have to pay the price.

PERCULUM EST EMPTORIS

If the object had been damaged or destroyed during the period between the sale and delivery as the result of a fact outside the seller's liability, i.e. by *casus fortuitus* or *vis major*, the risk in the thing sold is borne by the buyer. That is to say that the seller was released of his duty to deliver, but the duty of the purchaser to pay the price was unaffected.

The rule *periculum est emptoris* applied once the contract of sale was *perfecta*, i.e. from the moment the parties have agreed to buy and to sell a specific object at a specific price and no suspensive condition appeared in the contract. Since ownership did not pass until delivery, the *periculum est emptoris* rule deviates from the general principle *res perit domino*, i.e. the owner has to bear the loss if an object is destroyed, damaged or deteriorates by *vis major* or *casus fortuitus*.

On the other hand, since the buyer bears the risk, he is entitled to all accretions to the thing before delivery.

The risk does not pass to the buyer upon the conclusion of the contract, where the parties have made an agreement to the contrary.

GUARANTEE AGAINST LATENT DEFECTS AND DICTA ET PROMISSA

It is difficult to define a latent defect but it is often described as being a defect which renders the object sold unfit for its ordinary or contemplated purpose.

With the *actio empti* the vendor could be held liable if he did not fulfill his part of the contract in good faith. This implies that the vendor could be held liable with the *actio empti* for damages, if he did not disclose a defect known to him but of which the buyer was not aware.

It could be difficult for the purchaser to establish the vendor's knowledge.

During the republican erathe *aediles curules* introduced special provisions in their edict, in respect of public sales of slaves and *iumenta*, beasts of draught and burden.

Originally these provisions were restricted to sales of slaves and *iumenta* in the market, but gradually the measure was extended to the sale of slaves and *pecora*, cattle outside the market, while Justinian finally declared the aedilitician ruling to be applicable to all sales irrespective of where they had taken place.

The original aedilitician provisions obliged the vendor to declare publicly certain defects, namely *morbi et vitia*, in the sense of temporary or permanent physical and mental defects; in respect of slaves the vendor must declare that *fugitivus errove sit noxaeve solutus non sit*, that he was not a runaway, nor a roamer and that he was free from noxal liability. If the vendor had not declared any of these defects at the conclusion of the contract of sale and if the slave or head of cattle had any of these defects, the buyer had the choice of two aedilitician actions. This meant that the *aediles curules* did not introduce the liability of the seller for latent defects in the object sold. The edict forced the seller to declare certain defects and granted the buyer a remedy in cases where such a defect existed and the seller had not brought it to the notice of the buyer.

However, the development of the aedilitician measure was such, that eventually, only in cases of latent defects the buyer could institute an action. This meant that if the buyer had been aware of the defect, or if the defect was such that everybody (except the buyer) would have noticed it, no aedilitician action was available.

The aedilitician actions could also be instituted by the buyer against the seller if the object sold was different from *quod dictum promissumve fuit*, what the seller declared and promised. The distinction between *dicta* and *promissa* is not very clear; both were verbal declarations claiming that some quality was present or lacking in the thing sold. The seller who was aware of the defect in the thing sold and did not disclose it to the buyer at the conclusion of the sale, as well as the seller who made fraudulent *dicta et promissa*, could be held liable by the buyer with the *actio empti* for damages.

The final aedilitician actions were the *actio redhibitoria*, which action was aimed at rescission of the sale and prescribed in six months, or secondly, the *actio quanti minoris*.

This last action had to be instituted within one year after the sale. The buyer claimed a reduction in the purchase price. Justinian made the *actio empti* available to the buyer to enforce the aedilitician provisions and in this way made the aedilitician actions virtually superfluous. The duties of the vendor were the rights of the buyer. The buyer could enforce his personal rights with personal actions, namely the *actio empti* or the *actio redhibitoria* or *actio quanti minoris*.

34. Conditional sales

The parties could include any condition into the contract of sale. There were a number of agreements which were commonly invoked.

IN DIEM ADDICTIO

The parties had agreed that the vendor reserved the right to cancel the contract of sale, if he received, within a given time, a better offer by a third party. As a rule, it was also agreed that he had to give the first buyer the opportunity to match the second offer. The *in diem addictio* was usually construed as a resolutive condition, but could be formulated as a suspensive condition.

LEX COMMISSORIA

This was a clause which reserved to the vendor the right to cancel the contract of sale, if the buyer did not pay the price by a certain time.

The *lex commissoria* was usually formulated resolutively.

PACTUM DISPLICENTIAE

This pact gave the buyer the right to return the object sold and demand his money back, if the object which he had received on approval did not satisfy him. The *pactum displicentiae* could be suspensive or resolutive.

PACTUM DE RETROVENDENDO

The parties had agreed that the vendor had the right to buy back the thing sold within a given time or at the occurrence of a certain event. This pact was resolutive. Regarding the manner of enforcement of these pacts, there was a conflict of opinion. The sources mention the *actiones empti et venditi* or *actiones in factum* and in some cases even the *reivindicatio*.

35. Locatio et conductio

Locatio et conductio, the contract of letting and hiring, or lease. A contract of lease was concluded as soon as the parties had reached agreement regarding three *essentialia*, viz to let and to hire, the subject-matter and the price.

As was the case with sale, the agreement could be reached in any manner. Firstly, the parties had to agree that one person wished to hire and another wished to let. Cf *Error in negotio*.

Secondly the parties had to agree on the subject-matter of the lease.

Depending on what was being let and hired the contract could be divided into three categories, namely, the *locatio conductio rei*, the letting and hiring of a thing, the *locatio conductio operarum*, the letting and hiring of services, and the *locatio conductio operis*, the letting and hiring of a piece of work to be done.

Thirdly, the parties had to agree on the price, *pretium* or *merces*. The price had to be in money. Ohterwise the transaction would be a *nudum pactum* which became actionable only in Justinian law. There was, however, one exception to this rule, the so-called *colonia partiaria*, where the rent consisted of a fixed quantity or a proportion of the produce of the let agricultural land.

The price had to be fixed, *merces certa* or *pretium certum*. The same difference of opinion and solution regarding the question whether the price could be fixed by a third party or not existed, as was the case in the contract of sale.

Locatio et conductio is a bilateral contract, i.e. two obligations arise; both parties to the contract of lease have a personal right against the other party and both parties have a duty against the other party. The contract is aimed at an exchange of performances. This contract developed from the *ius gentium* and was therefore, based on the *bona fides*. Consequently, the duties of both parties were defined by the requirements of good faith.

36. Locatio conductio rei

Locatio conductio rei was the contract of letting and hiring of an object. The object had to be specific and *in commercio*. The thing let should also, in principle, be *res non consumptibilis*, things not consumed by use, but *res consumptibiles* could be let *ad pompam et ostentationem*, for display.

Furthermore, any object movable or immovable, corporeal or incorporeal, could be let. There was no requirement that the object let had to be the property of the lessor; thus, it was possible to let another's property.

DUTIES OF THE HIRER

Firstly, the *conductor*, hirer or lessee, had to pay the rent to the lessor. In principle the rent was due after the lessor had made the object available to the hirer. Secondly, the lessee had to return the thing at the end of the letting to the *locator*, lessor.

During his tenure of the thing the hirer had to show the care of a *bonus paterfamilias*, which meant that he was liable for *dolus* and *culpa levis in abstracto*. In other words, if the object let were destroyed or damaged during the *conductor's* tenure, as the result of his intent or negligence, the conductor was liable for damages; that is, the lessor, *locator*, could institute the *actio locati* for the loss suffered by him. If on the other hand, the object let was destroyed or damaged during the hirer's tenure without his fault, i.e. by *casus fortuitus* or *vis major*, the lessor carried the risk, *periculum est locatoris*, in that the hirer was relieved of his liability for the rent for the period of non-enjoyment.

Periculum est locatoris means that if without the fault of either party the hirer was prevented from enjoyment of the object let, he was released from his duty to pay the rent.

The duties of the hirer are the rights of the lessor. The lessor could enforce his personal rights with a personal action, namely the *actio locati.*

DUTIES OF THE LESSOR

The first duty of the lessor was *frui licere praestare*, he had to give undisturbed enjoyment of the thing let to the lessee.

This implies that he had to make the *res* available to the hirer. The physical control provided to the hirer was, however, unprotected, *detentio*. The lessor was the protected *possessor.*

The second implication of *frui licere praestare* was that the lessor had to ensure undisturbed enjoyment. This in its turn meant that the lessor had a duty to keep the object in good condition and furthermore, that he had the duty to protect the hirer's tenure.

The hirer only had a personal right against the lessor. Hence, if the hirer's tenure and enjoyment was interfered with by third parties, the hirer had to go to the lessor, who had the duty to protect the hirer's tenure.

Consequently a further duty of the lessor was to guarantee against eviction.

GUARANTEE AGAINST EVICTION

Eviction took place where the hirer lost possession of the object let, as the result of an *actio in rem* being instituted against him.

In this case of eviction the lessor was always liable (even without *dolus* or *culpa* on his side) and had to pay damages to the lessee.

CONTRACTUAL LIABILITY AND RISK

Lease being a *bonae fidei* contract, the lessor, during the conclusion of the contract, had to act in good faith. In Justinian law this meant that the lessor was liable for *dolus* and *culpa levis in abstracto*. In other words, if the hirer were to suffer damages through fraud or negligence on the part of the lessor, the hirer could institute the *actio conducti* and hold the lessor liable for these damages.

Once the contract was concluded, the lessor remained liable for *dolus* and *culpa levis in abstracto*. This entailed that where the hirer was prevented from enjoyment of the object let, as the result of fraud or negligence on the part of the lessor, the *actio conducti* for damages was at the disposal of the hirer.

If the hirer did not have use and quiet enjoyment of the object let, regardless of the reason, he did not have to pay the rent, which meant that the risk was carried by the lessor, *periculum est locatoris*.

Finally, the lessor had the duty to accept the thing back at the expiry of the lease and to reimburse the hirer for any necessary expenses incurred in maintaining the thing.

For other expenses incurred the hirer had a *ius tollendi*.

The duties of the lessor are the rights of the lessee. The lessee could enforce his personal rights with a personal action namely, the *actio conducti*.

If the lessor sold or donated or disposed in any other manner and transferred the ownership of the thing let, the new owner could evict the lessee by way of his *reivindicatio*, even if the agreed period of lease had not yet expired.

The hirer did not have a real right in the object let but only a personal right against the lessor. Hence, he did not have a defence against the *reivindicatio*, but could claim damages from the lessor with his *actio conducti*.

TERMINATION OF LEASE

As a rule, a contract of *locatio conductio rei* was for a specific period, i.e. a resolutive term was entered into the contract. If no such term was agreed upon, either party could terminate the contract unilaterally.

37. Locatio conductio operarum

Locatio conductio operarum was the letting of one's services. This was a contract of minor importance in a society where slavery played an important role.

The labourer let *operas suas*, his services, and was therefore the lessor, *locator*, and could claim his wages with the *actio locati*.

The employer was the hirer, *conductor*, and could claim the services with the *actio conducti*.

38. Locatio conductio operis

Locatio conductio operis was the letting and hiring of a piece of work. The contract was concluded as soon as the parties had reached agreement regarding the following three points, viz to let and to hire, the *opus*, the work, and the *merces*, the price.

As mentioned previously, agreement could be reached in any manner.

The *opus*, the work to be done generally required a certain expertise or a special capacity, for example *insulam aedificandam locare*, building a block of flats, the cartage of goods, the carriage of a passenger, the cleaning or repairing of clothes, etc.

The *merces* had to be a specific sum of money.

The party contracting to do the work was the *conductor*, the hirer or independent contractor, since he hired the *opus*, while the party commissioning the work was the *locator*, the lessor, since he let the work.

DUTIES OF THE CONDUCTOR

Firstly, the contractor had the duty of *opus facere*, to produce the specified result. Since the *conductor* was responsible for the finished product the question of his liability deserves attention. During the conclusion and execution of the contract, the contractor was liable for *dolus* and *culpa levis in abstracto*, while *imperitia*, lack of expertise, was considered to be *culpa*. This means that if the failure to produce the agreed result could be attributed to the fraud or negligence of the contractor, he was liable for damages by way of the *actio locati*.

There are, however, texts that indicate that some contractors in certain cases were held liable for *casus* or even *vis major*.

Since the contract was based on the *bona fides*, the *locator* was not bound to pay the *merces* in cases where the specified result was not produced as the result of a fact which fell within the liability of the contractor.

It is, however, difficult to formulate a general rule relating to risk, since the texts on this topic are contradictory. The final duty of the contractor was to take care of things entrusted to him. In classical law the contractor was liable for *custodia* with regard to things entrusted to him by the *lessor*. Even in Justinian law some contractors were held liable for *custodia* in this regard.

DUTY OF THE LOCATOR

The *lessor's* chief duty was to pay the contractor his remuneration.

LEX RHODIA DE IACTU

A particular feature of carriage by sea effected by *locatio conductio operis* was the *Lex Rhodia de iactu*. If the master of the ship was forced to jettison some of the cargo, the loss was to be shared among the consigners and the ship's master, in proportion to their interest in the whole.

39. Societas

Societas, the partnership-contract, was concluded when the parties had reached agreement on certain *essentialia*, viz to pool resources and to pursue a common profitable goal.

The agreement could be reached in any manner, as was the case in all consensual contracts.

Each partner was then required to make a contribution. What they brought into the partnership could differ in nature, for example money, property, services, as well as value. The goal pursued by the partnership could not be illegal, impossible or immoral and had to be to the mutual advantage of the partners.

Depending on the way in which the common purpose was pursued, various types of partnership contracts could be distinguished.

Societas omnium bonorum was the partnership contract, in which all the partners pooled their assets. The assets became joint property and everything subsequently acquired also became joint property.

Societas quaestus was a partnership contract according to which everything the partners acquired from both business or professional activities, fell into the partnership.

Societas unius or *alicuius negotii* or *negotiationis* was the partnership contract aimed at conducting one particular type of business.

Societas unius rei, the partnership contract for the exploitation of a single joint asset.

The *societas* was no legal person. This implies that the *societas* could not be owner or *possessor* of a thing, the *societas* could not be debtor or creditor, the *societas* could not litigate, buy or sell, hire or let etc.

Societas was a bilateral contract, i.e. each partner had personal rights against the other partners, but all the partners had duties against each other. The rights and duties of all the partners were similar.

The contract had its roots in the *ius gentium* and was consequently based on the *bona fides*. The duties of the parties were, therefore, defined by the requirements of good faith.

DUTIES OF THE PARTNERS

The first duty of each partner was to make his contribution. This could be done in various ways, for example, transfer of ownership to the other partners. However, it was also possible to retain the ownership and to place the object in question at the disposal of the other partners.

COMMUNICARE LUCRUM ET DAMNUM

The principal duty of each partner, consisted of *communicare lucrum et damnum*, to share the profit and loss. Unless a different agreement had been reached, every partner was entitled to an equal share in the benefits which accrued as a result of the partnership's activities and every partner had a duty to reimburse the other partners their share with regard to costs and losses.

In the absence of other arrangements in the partnership contract, regarding the sharing of profits and losses, equality of shares was the rule, even if the various contributions were not equal. However, any other arrangement could be agreed upon, except the *societas leonina*, in which it was agreed that one partner would not have a share in the profits. In such a case no *societas* would have been concluded, since the essence of the contract was the mutual advantage of the parties.

CONTRACTUAL LIABILITY

Since *societas* was based on the *bona fides* the parties had to act in good faith. In Justinian law this meant that each partner was liable for *dolus* and *culpa levis in concreto*. This meant that each partner had to show, with regard to the activities of the partnership, the same degree of care that he would show in his own affairs. In the other partners suffered losses as the result of one partner's *dolus* or *culpa levis in concreto*, they could institute the *actio pro socio* against him for damages.

The duties of the one partner are the personal rights of the other partner. Each partner had the same rights and duties against the other partners. Each partner could enforce his personal rights with a personal action, the *actio pro socio*. A partner condemned in the action became *infamis*, since he had betrayed the trust placed upon him.

When a partner entered into a legal act with a third party, that legal act only had effect as far as the parties participating in it, were concerned; the other partners were unaffected by such acts. However, if the act was entered into for the partnership's business the partners had the duty of *communicare lucrum et damnum*. Although the partner in question had acquired rights and/or incurred liabilities for himself, the other partners were entitled to their share in the assets and were liable to him to share the liabilities.

In other words, in Roman law one partner did not represent the others and the Roman law of *societas* was that of the relations of the partners *inter se*, among themselves.

TERMINATION OF THE PARTNERSHIP

Each partner could unilaterally dissolve the partnership contract. However, if he gave *intempestive*, at a bad time, or *dolo malo*, fraudulent, notice, the other partners could hold him liable for damages with the *actio pro socio*.

Since the partnership was originally highly personal, death, *capitis deminutio* or insolvency of one of the partners dissolved the *societas*.

Originally the bringing of the *actio pro socio* also dissolved a *societas* but in later law this action could be instituted *manente societate*.

Furthermore, a *societas* would end if the period agreed upon expired, if its goal had been achieved, or the communal property was destroyed.

40. Mandatum

Mandatum, the contract of mandate was concluded as soon as the parties had reached agreement that the one person (the *mandatarius*, the mandatary) would gratuitously perform acts for another person (the *mandator*, mandator).

Agreement could be reached in any manner and the gratuitous nature of the contract distinguished it from *locatio conductio operis*. It was essentially the doing of a favour for a friend and a Roman felt it his duty to help his friends free of charge. However, it became accepted practice to pay professional people who practised the *artes liberales* a *honorarium* or *salarium* and the agreed *honorarium* could be claimed by *cognitio extraordinaria*.

The service requested under a mandate could be anything: any factual act, any legal act, a single act or a general administration of one's affairs as long as it was not illegal, impossible or immoral.

The mandate had to be in the interest of the mandator or in the interest of a third party, but a purported mandate in the interest of the mandatory only, the *mandatum tua gratia* was ineffective and considered to be advice which did not constitute an obligation.

The *mandatum pecuniae credendae*, a mandate to lend money to a third party was a form of informal suretyship, where the main debtor had to be sued first.

Mandatum is an imperfectly bilateral contract, that had its roots in the *ius gentium* and was based on the *bona fides*. In short, the duties of the parties were defined by the requirements of good faith.

DUTIES OF THE MANDATORY

The first duty of the mandatory was to carry out the mandate.

If anything was acquired under the mandate, the mandatory had the duty to transfer it to the mandator.

He was liable for *dolus* and *culpa levis in abstracto*, which meant that he had to perform his task like a *bonus paterfamilias.* If the mandator suffered loss, which could be attributed to the fraud or negligence of the mandatory, he could claim damages with the *actio mandati.*

The duties of the mandatory are the rights of the mandator. He could enforce his personal rights with a personal action, the *actio mandati.*

The possibility exists that the mandatory has a counterclaim, namely if he incurred expenses and/or suffered financial loss in the performance of the contract. In that case, he could institute the *actio mandati contraria* against the mandator.

The mandatory did not represent the mandator. Where the mandatory entered into a legal act with a third party, only the parties involved were affected by the act. Thus, the mandator was not directly affected by any acts the mandatory performed.

TERMINATION OF MANDATE

Carrying out of the mandate is the most obvious manner in which to terminate a mandate. Furthermore, either party could renounce the contract as long as *res adhuc integra*, i.e. while execution of the mandate had not yet started.

Finally, death of either party, a resolutive term or condition also terminated the contract.

41. Quasi contractus

Quasi contractus are those lawful acts which constitute an obligation although not founded on agreement. The most important quasi contracts are *negotiorum gestio, tutela* and *solutio indebiti.*

Negotiorum gestio takes place if one person (i.e. *negotiorum gestor*) performs some service for another, (i.e. *dominus negotii*) without agreement between the parties.

The relationship between the parties created obligations which did not derive from agreement but equally were not created by wrongful conduct and broadly speaking was analogous to *mandatum.*

The service performed could be anything: any factual act, any legal act, a single act or a general administration of one's affairs, as long as it was not illegal, impossible or immoral.

The *gestor* had to have the *animus aliena negotia gerenda*, the intention to manage another's affairs. The *negotia* had to be *utiliter gesta*, in the interest of the *dominus*. It was not necessary for the result to be successful and if the service was reasonable when undertaken, *utiliter coeptum*, the fact that the *dominus* did not derive benefit from it, was irrelevant.

Negotiorum gestio is an imperfectly bilateral quasi contract that derived from the *ius honorarium* and was consequently based on the *bona fides*.

DUTIES OF THE GESTOR

The *gestor* had to deliver any proceeds to the *dominus*.

Furthermore, even though he acted gratuitously, the *gestor* was liable for *dolus* and *culpa levis in abstracto*, which meant that he had to perform the undertaking like a *bonus paterfamilias*. Cf *Mandatum*.

The duties of the *gestor* are the rights of the *dominus*. He could enforce his personal rights with a personal action, the *actio negotiorum gestorum directa*.

The possibility exists that the *gestor* has a counterclaim, namely, if he incurred expenses and/or suffered financial loss in the completion of the task. In that case he could institute the *actio negotiorum gestorum contraria* against the *dominus*.

The *gestor* did not represent the *dominus*.

Justinian's Institutes mention the following quasi contract: *tutela*, the relationship between *tutor* and word; *communio*, the relationship between joint owners; *legatum*, the relationship between an heir and a legatee, and *solutio indebiti*.

It is, however, incorrect to limit the number of quasi contracts, because every situation which creates an obligation which does not qualify as a contract or a delict, is a quasi contract.

In this context the quasi-contractual *condictiones* were relevant.

42. Quasi contractual condictiones

The *condictio* was an *actio in personam* deriving from the *strictum ius* by which the plaintiff claimed that ownership of a specific thing or quantity thereof, or a specific sum of money, had to be passed to him by the defendant.

The *condictio* was used to enforce *stipulatio* and *mutuum* and was also made available in special cases where it would have been unfair if ownership had not been transferred. In these cases the *condictio* derived from quasi contract and the claim was based on the principle that it is inequitable that one person should be enriched to the detriment of another. The most important quasi contractual *condictiones* were:

CONDICTIO INDEBITI

Where a person erroneously believed that he owed something to another party and consequently performed in discharge of this imaginary duty, he was entitled to recover the same by means of the *condictio indebiti.*

The plaintiff had to be labouring under a mistake and must have performed *per errorem*, in error. If he made an undue performance knowingly, his action was regarded as a donation.

The other party who received the money or property had to be *bona fide*, i.e. he must have believed that the performance was due to him. A *mala fide* recipient would have been committing *furtum*, theft. Furthermore, ownership must have been transferred by one of the derivative modes of acquisition. Finally, there had to be no existing debt. In these circumstances the person who made the undue performance could institute the *condictio indebiti* against the receiver. He claimed recovery of the same thing or the same quantity of the same kind and quality.

CONDICTIO CAUSA DATA CAUSA NON SECUTA
Where a person transferred ownership for a purpose which did not result, he was entitled to reclaim what was given, by means of this *condictio*.

CONDICTIO OB TURPEM VEL INIUSTAM CAUSAM
Where a person transferred ownership as the result of an illegal or immoral *causa*, this *condictio* was available to reclaim what had been paid or delivered. However, the plaintiff had to be free of *turpitudo*, guilt.

CONDICTIO SINE CAUSA
A post-classical *condictio* covering the same field as the previous *condictiones*, but also available in some cases where ownership had been transferred without a reason.

43. Contractus innominati

Roman law recognized only a limited number of contracts. While any lawful undertaking could be made binding, by means of *stipulatio*, some common daily transactions which fell outside the normal categories of contracts were gradually rendered enforceable. By the time of Justinian, there was another category of contracts, the *contractus innominati*, the unnamed contracts. The essence of these transactions was the agreement between two parties that each should perform something to the other, i.e. *quid pro quo*.

According to the nature of the mutual performances, four different forms were distinguished:

DO UT DES

I give, in order that you should give. *Permutatio*, the agreement of exchange or barter.

DO UT FACIAS

I give, in order that you should do.

FACIO UT FACIAS

I do, in order that you should do. *Aestimatum*, the agreement of hawking.

FACIO UT DES

I do, in order that you should give.

Such agreements were merely *nuda pacta* and no obligations arose. Therefore, neither party had an enforceable right against the other.

If, however, one of the parties had performed his side of the arrangement and the other party did not reciprocate, the first party would not have an action to enforce effecting of the transaction in full. In certain cases he could recover his own performance by means of the *condictio causa data causa non secuta* or with the *actio doli*.

In other cases the *praetor* introduced an *actio in factum*, by means of which the party who had honoured his undertaking could force the other party to carry out his part of the agreement.

Justinian made the *actio praescriptis verbis* available in all such cases. This implies that every agreement for mutual performance became recognized as a *contractus* upon part performance. *Contractus innominati* were, therefore, constituted by agreement plus part performance.

44. Pacta

Consensus, agreement, in itself was a mere *pactum, pactio* or *conventio*, pact, and not actionable. *Ex nudo pacto non oritur actio*, from a mere agreement no action arises. Nevertheless, this general principle was not strictly adhered to in Roman law and gradually some *pacta* became actionable, i.e. gave rise to an action and therefore to an obligation.

These pacta were classified as follows:

PACTA ADIECTA

Pacta adiecta were agreements made in connection with a contract. If made at the time of the original contract (i.e. a *pactum in continenti*) they were enforceable by the relevant contractual action. Any *pactum* made in connection with a contract could be invoked as a defence, if necessary by an express *exceptio pacti conventi.*

PACTA PRAETORIA

These were *pacta* made enforceable by the *praetor*. The most important among them were *constitutum debiti*, an agreement to pay your own or another's debt at an agreed time; *receptum arbitri*, the undertaking to act as arbitrator in a dispute; *receptum argentarii*, an undertaking by a banker to be liable for his client's obligation and *receptum nautarum, cauponum, stabulariorum*, the undertaking of the ship's master, innkeeper and liveryman that their customer's goods would be safe.

PACTA LEGITIMA

Pacta made enforceable by imperial *constitutiones*. Examples are *pactum dotis*, the agreement to give a dowry and *pactum donationis*, the agreement to make a gift.

45. Donation

Donatio, gift, is any legal act, whatever its nature, whereby someone gratuitously enriches another at the expense of himself. This entails that the donor has the *animus donandi*, the intention to make a gift. Examples of donations are the transfer of ownership by way of *mancipatio, in iure cessio* or *traditio*, release from a debt, grant of a servitude or usufruct over the property of the donor, payment of another's debt, *stipulatio donandi causa*, a stipulation whereby a gift was promised.

Justinian made the *pactum donationis*, the agreement to make a gift, actionable. In Roman law, gifts between the living were governed by various rules. For example the ban on gifts between husband and wife.

46. Suretyship

In many cases where a person desires credit the other party will only grant credit if security for the discharge of the debt is provided. Security can be either real or personal, i.e. suretyship.

Suretyship is a contract whereby a third party (i.e. the surety) binds himself to the creditor for performance of another's debt. This means that the creditor, apart from his personal right against the original debtor, acquires a second personal right against the surety. The surety is liable with his whole estate, but not for more than the principal debt. Suretyship was important in Rome, since the Romans felt it their duty to help a friend by acting as his surety. Moreover, personal security was preferred over real security for a variety of reasons, of which the effective execution of judgment on the person of the judgment debtor was not the least.

Suretyship could be effected informally by way of *mandatum pecuniae credendae, constitutum debiti alieni* or *receptum argentarii.*

Formal suretyship was always constituted by *stipulatio: Idem dari spondes? Spondeo; Idem fide promittis? Fide promitto; Id tua fide esse iubesne? Jubeo.*

The three forms of formal suretyship were derived from the word 'promise': *sponsio, fidepromissio* and *fideiussio.* During early classical law *fideiussio* became the usual form of suretyship.

FIDEIUSSIO

All types of obligations could be guaranteed by way of *fideiussio.* The liability of a *fideiussor* was transmissible to his heirs.

Since the surety undertook the same obligation as the principal debtor, any of them could be sued for the whole of what was due. The creditor could proceed against any of them but, as a result of the effect of *litiscontestatio* he had only one opportunity.

The surety who paid could recover from the principal debtor with the *actio mandati contraria.*

Gradually measures were introduced to improve the position of the *fideiussor.*

BENEFICIUM DIVISIONIS

The benefit of division applies when several people have become surety for the same debt. Hadrian provided that a *fideiussor* who was sued by the creditor, could claim that this liability be limited to the amount of debt divided by the number of solvent sureties.

BENEFICIUM CEDENDARUM ACTIONUM

This was the benefit of cession of actions whereby a surety could demand that the creditor who proceeded against him, cede all remedies in respect of the claim to him. This enables the surety to proceed against the principal debtor by way of these remedies and improves his recourse.

BENEFICIUM EXCUSSIONIS OR ORDINIS OR DISCUSSIONIS

The benefit of excussion was introduced by Justinian who provided that the main debtor had to be sued first. The surety, if proceeded against by the creditor, could require that the creditor should first sue the debtor for performance or payment. If his claim was not fully satisfied the creditor could claim from the surety.

This, in itself logical principle, was impossible in classical law as a result of the effect of *litiscontestatio*, namely, extinguishing the obligation. Justinian abolished this rule where there were several debtors and thus made the *beneficium excussionis* possible.

Abovementioned benefits can be renounced by the surety either expressly or impliedly.

The *Senatus Consultum Velleianum* prohibited women *intercedere pro alio*, i.e. assuming liability for others. If the woman was sued on such a transaction, the *praetor* gave her the *exceptio Senatus Consulti Velleiani.*

The *Authentica si qua mulier* forbade *intercessio* by a wife on behalf of her husband. Such guarantee was void.

47. Delictum

An obligation arises from a contract or a *quasi* contract, from a delict or a *quasi* delict.

Delict and *quasi* delict are wrongful acts which create an obligation between the victim and the wrongdoer.

The victim (i.e. creditor) had a personal action against the wrongdoer (i.e. debtor); by way of this action he claimed either a *poena*, a monetary penalty, or an amount of money in which his patrimonial loss as well as the penalty were accounted for. Examples of the first type of action, the *actio poenalis*, were the *actio furti* and the *actio iniuriarum.* If, however, the victim had suffered financial loss as the result of the delict, as was the case in *furtum*, it was possible to institute an *actio rei persecutoria* as well as the *actio poenalis.* An *actio rei persecutoria* purported to replace the victim in the financial position wherein he should have been.

The second type of action, the so-called *actio mixta* was, as the name denotes, a mixture of an *actio poenalis* and an *actio rei persecutoria.* This means that in such a case the victim had only one action against the wrongdoer. The most important example of the *actio mixta* was the *actio legis Aquiliae*, whereby the victim claimed patrimonial loss as well as punishment from the wrongdoer.

All these actions were instituted by the victim himself in civil proceedings. In this regard the Roman law of delict also served the function of modern criminal law. In Rome the scope of criminal law was restricted to *crimina publica*, crimes against the state or society, e.g. murder, high treason, sacrilege. The perpetrator of a crime of this nature was prosecuted under criminal law and punished with the death penalty, exile, imprisonment, corporal punishment or a fine.

Delicta privata, however, were wrongs against the individual, his family or his property. The original redress was *talio*, retaliation, an eye for an eye, a tooth for a tooth. Gradually retaliation was avoided by agreeing to pay compensation and increasing intervention by the state. Thus, the victim of the wrong had to institute his personal action (*poenalis* or *mixta*) in civil proceedings to recover a monetary penalty as compensation (by way of an *actio poenalis*) or an amount of money calculated to redress the patrimonial loss suffered by the victim, as well as to punish the wrongdoer.

This particular function of the delictual action explains the following peculiarities: Delictual liability was cumulative. Thus if several people had participated in a delict, each was liable in full and atonement by one did not release the others.

Secondly, delictual actions were not passively transmissible. Thus, liability for a delict ended with the death of the perpetrator.

48. Elements of delictual liability

As has been said, a delict (and a *quasi* delict) were wrongful acts which created an obligation between the victim and the wrongdoer.

This, however, does not imply that every wrongful conduct whereby a person caused harm to property or personality gave rise to an obligation. Only a limited series of individual delicts gave rise to an obligation, i.e. to an *actio in personam*. The Roman *delicta privata* developed casuistically and the Roman lawyers did not conceive an abstract concept of delict. Nevertheless, the elements of delictual liability have their roots in Roman law:

ACT

Originally, the acts which constituted delictual liability were all positive acts which directly caused harm to property or personality. However, with regard to wrongful damage to property as introduced by the *Lex Aquila* the praetorian extensions broadened the application of the provisions of the *Lex* to indirect causation during classical law. In Justinian law, in exceptional circumstances, even an omission could give rise to an action derived from the *Lex Aquilia*.

UNLAWFULNESS

The act had to be *iniuria*, contrary to law, *quod non iure factum est, hoc est contra ius*, that what is not done lawfully, i.e. what is contrary to law. Despite the fact that the act was contrary to statutory or customary law there were recognized defences which exempted liability, for example necessity.

HARM

The wrongful conduct of the defendant had to cause injury to property or personality.

CAUSATION

Between the act of the wrongdoer and the harm to the victim there has to be a causal link, in short the damage or injury must be the direct result of the act of the defendant. The Roman lawyers did not formulate doctrines, but achieved remarkable result with common sense.

MENS REA

Mens rea, the mental element of delict, denotes the mental attitude of the offender. Originally *mens rea* was not expressly required for delictual liability in primitive Roman law, since the delicts which led to liability required deliberate conduct. Someone causing harm to property or personality of another was held liable, because experience taught that people who commit certain harmful acts, as a rule, intend to cause harm.

Gradually, however, intent became an explicit requirement for all delictual liability.

Negligence constituted liability only under the *lex Aquilia*. However, the principle that there should be no liability without negligence derives from Roman law.

49. Furtum

Furtum is generally translated as theft, but the Roman concept of *furtum* was much wider than theft, as the pledgee or depositee who used the pledged or deposited thing committed *furtum* and even the owner who removed the pledged thing from the pledgee without having discharged the debt for which the thing was given as security, committed *furtum*. Therefore, *furtum* was an extensive and vague notion.

This is also exemplified by the fact that Gaius did not attempt to define *furtum* but warned that *furtum* was not limited to the carrying off of another's thing, but *'generaliter cum quis rem alienam invito domino contrectat*, in general where someone uses a thing contrary to the wish of the owner.

A definition of *furtum* is found in the Digest: *Furtum est contrectatio rei fraudulosa lucri faciendi gratia vel etiam usus eius possessionisve*, theft is the fraudulent interference with a thing, whether with the thing itself, or the use or possession of it for the purpose of gain.

THE ELEMENTS OF FURTUM

The first requirement was *contrectatio*, the using of an object contrary to the wish of the owner, or the person who had an interest in the thing. Examples are, the removal of property, receiving of stolen goods, accepting a *solutio indebiti* in bad faith, hiding an escaped slave, selling a pledged object without being entitled to do so by way of a *pactum distrahendi* etc.

Secondly, the mental element of *furtum* arises. Since *furtum* required deliberate conduct, it is clear that intent was postulated. Expressions used in the texts such as *animus furandi* or *adfectus furandi, fraudulosa, lucri faciendi gratia* all refer to this requirement. Cf Gaius 3, 197: *Furtum sine dolo malo non committitur*, theft cannot be committed without intent.

Finally, the stolen thing had to be a movable and tangible object. Originally doubt existed regarding this fact, but at an early stage it became settled that there could be no theft of immovables. In most cases *furtum* was committed against somebody else's property, nevertheless *furtum* of your own property was possible.

VARIOUS TYPES OF FURTUM

The most important distinction which was made by the Twelve Tables was between *furtum manifestum* and *furtum nec manifestum*.

Furtum manifestum, manifest theft, was to be caught in the act. Originally differing views of what this meant, existed. Did the thief have to be caught red-handed, or was it sufficient if the thief was caught on the premises where the theft was committed, or even where the thief was arrested with the stolen property before he had moved it to its intended hiding place? Justinian law adopted all three abovementioned cases as *furtum manifestum*.

According to the Twelve Tables a *fur manifestus*, manifest thief, who defended himself with arms, or who stole by night, could be killed. In all other cases he was brought before a *magistratus*, flogged and allocated to the person he had wronged. The penalties prescribed under the Twelve Tables, fell into disuse as the *praetor* introduced the *actio furti manifesti*, a penal action for four times the value of the stolen thing.

In all cases which did not qualify as *furtum manifestum* the thief was *nec manifestus*, non-manifest, and the *actio furti nec manifesti*, a penal action for double the value of the object was instituted for the punishment of the thief.

The following distinction was also made. *Furtum rei vel usus possessionisve. Furtum rei* was the intentional and unlawful appropriation of another's movable property.

Furtum usus was improper use of a thing by the possessor. The 'thief' was lawfully in possession of the object, but handled it in an unlawful manner.

Furtum possessionis was the appropriation of possession by the owner. The owner removed his property unlawfully from the lawful possession of another.

Once all the elements of *furtum* were present, an obligation arose between the thief and his victim, i.e. the creditor, who had a personal right against the thief, i.e. debtor, which was enforced by a personal action, the *actio furti*.

WHO COULD INSTITUTE THE ACTIO FURTI?

Originally the *actio furti* could only be instituted by the owner of the stolen object. However, in later law the action became available to any person who had an interest in the non-disappearance of the thing. This applied firstly to anyone liable for *custodia* in classical law, but there were other interested parties against whom theft could be committed, such as a pledgee, usufructuary, *bona fide possessor* etc. In a case where the *actio furti* was instituted by a person with an interest in the thing, an action by the owner was in principle precluded.

AGAINST WHOM COULD THE ACTIO FURTI BE INSTITUTED?

Firstly, the thief and his accomplices, i.e. the person or persons who actually committed the *contrectatio* were held liable. The liability was cumulative, i.e. the creditor could claim the full amount from each debtor with the *actio furti manifesti* (four times the value) or the *actio furti nec manifesti* (twice the value of the object stolen) and each wrongdoer had to pay the full amount.

Accessories, i.e. those who had assisted the thief *ope et consilio*, by aid and counsel, were also held liable to the *actio furti nec manifesti.*

The *actio furti* was an *actio poenalis*, a penal action, aimed at punishment of the wrongdoer and thus providing amends to the victim.

Moreover, the victim of *furtum* was usually deprived of his property and suffered pecuniary loss. Therefore, he could institute an *actio reipersecutoria* to recover the thing or his damages besides the *actio furti* to recover a penalty.

The most obvious action in this context was the *reivindicatio*, the *actio in rem* by means of which the owner reclaimed the possession of his property from whoever may have held it without right, irrespective whether such person was *bona fide* or *mala fide.*

If, however, the *reivindicatio* could not be instituted, because the object could not be found or had been consumed or destroyed, the owner could institute the *condictio furtiva* instead of the *reivindicatio.* This was a personal action by means of which the owner claimed the value of the thing from the thief or his heirs. Thus, the owner had either the *reivindicatio* or the *condictio furtiva*. In exceptional cases other *actiones rei persecutoriae*, for example the *actio depositi* could apply.

50. Rapina

Rapina, robbery, is theft with violence. Thus, the elements of *rapina* were essentially those of *furtum* plus the additional element of *vis*, violence.

Originally, *rapina* did not have a special action and the action that applied to *furtum* applied also to robbery. Since, as a rule, a robber is not caught in the act, the punishment for robbery was double the value of the object in case.

Towards the end of the republic robbery was on the increase and the *preator* gave a special action, the *actio vi bonorum raptorum* for four times the value of the thing.

WHO COULD INSTITUTE THE ACTIO VI BONORUM RAPTORUM?
The person who was robbed, i.e. the person in charge of the thing at the moment of *rapina.*

AGAINST WHOM COULD THE ACTIO VI BONORUM RAPTORUM BE INSTITUTED?
Against the robber and his accomplices. The liability was cumulative, i.e. each robber had to pay the full penalty.

The action had to instituted within a year, after that the action lay for the value of the object.

In classical law the *actio vi bonorum raptorum* was an *actio poenalis*, i.e. penal action aimed at punishment of the wrongdoer and thus providing amends to the victim. Thus the victim could institute an *actio rei persecutoria*, usually the *reivindicatio* or the *condictio furtiva*, beside the penal action. In Justinian law the *actio vi bonorum raptorum* became an *actio mixta*, in other words an action aimed not only at punishing the wrongdoer but at recovering the pecuniary loss in one claim. This in practice reduced the punishment to three times the value and the *reivindicatio* or *condictio furtiva* were thus excluded.

51. Damnum iniuria datum

Damnum iniuria datum, wrongful damage to property. This was and is the most important delict.

Damnum iniuria datum literally translated, damage wrongfully caused, is misleading, since Roman law did not have a general action for damages, caused by wrongful conduct, but provided actions for specific situations.

Originally, the Twelve Tables and other *leges* provided actions for several instances of wrongful damage to property. However, all these specific delicts were superseded by the *Lex Aquilia*, a *plebiscitum* of approximately 287 BC, which introduced a uniform delict of wrongful damage to property.

The *Lex Aquilia* was divided into three chapters:

Chapter 1 provided that whoever wrongfully slew the slave or a four-footed grazing animal of another, should be condemned to the owner for the highest value of the thing in the past year.

Chapter 2 dealt with an *adstipulator* and fell into desuetude.

Chapter 3 provided that if someone wrongfully burned, broke or fractured objects belonging (except slaves and *pecus* slain) to another, the wrongdoer should be condemned to the owner for the value of the thing in the past thirty days.

From the wording of the two relevant chapters it should be clear that the original Act was rather primitive, which resulted in a limited field of application.

Chapter 1 used the verb *occidere*, to slay, and therefore killing effected in another manner, in principle, fell outside the scope of the Act. Likewise the word *pecus*, a quadruped which grazes in herds was limited, since animals who were either not four-footed or who did not graze or did not graze in herds were excluded from the Act.

The wrongful wounding of a slave or a *pecus* was not dealt with.

Chapter 3 limited the modes of damaging another's property to burning, breaking and fracturing. All other forms of causing damage to property were thus excluded.

The *actio legis Aquiliae* was an *actio mixta* aimed, not only at recovering the damage suffered, but also punishing the wrongdoer. The *Lex Aquilia* attempted to achieve this by holding the wrongdoer liable for the highest value of the damaged property in the past year, as well as in the last 30 days respectively. Although this meant to punish the wrongdoer by making him pay more than the actual damages suffered, as well as to mete out a more severe punishment in cases falling under chapter 1, the practical result was contrary to this.

The acts leading to liability under the *Lex Aquilia* were direct positive acts, i.e. *occidere, urere, rumpere, frangere.* Thus, damage had to be caused directly by the wrongdoer, by means of a positive act. The Roman lawyers worded this requirement as *corpore datum*. Damage caused indirectly, or by way of omission, did not fall within the scope of the Act.

Moreover, a tangible thing had to be damaged, since only *res quae tangi possunt* can be slayed, burned, broken or fractured. The Roman lawyers worded this requirement as *damnum corpori*. Thus, patrimonial loss suffered without damage to a tangible thing was not included.

The *Lex Aquilia* only required wrongful damage and ignored the *mens rea* element. Therefore, originally Aquilian liability could be incurred without intent or negligence. Finally, the Aquilian action was available only to the owner, while other interested parties had no remedy.

From the above it should be clear that the original *Lex Aquilia* had a limited scope and left many instances of wrongful damage to property without legal redress.

Consequently, the *praetor*, the lawyers and Justinian extended the application of the provisions of the *lex*, to adapt to the requirements of a developed society.

With regard to the verb *occidere* used in chapter 1, the *praetor* extended the scope of the Act, by granting an *actio legis Aquiliae in factum* for *causam mortis praestare*, the causing of death.

The denomination *pecus* was interpreted widely to include among others pigs, elephants and camels.

The wrongful wounding of another's slave and *pecus*, as well as the wrongful killing or wounding of another's animals not included under *pecus*, was by way of interpretation brought under chapter 3.

A most important and daring feat of *interpretatio* was accomplished to extend the scope of chapter 3. *Ruptum enim intellegitur quoque modo corruptum*, in other words *rumpere* was interpreted as *corrumpere*. In reality *rumpere* is to break and *corrumpere* means to spoil, but the lawyers interpreted *rumpere* to include *corrumpere*, thus any form of damage directly caused by a positive act fell under chapter 3 accordingly. For example cutting, bruising, contusing, pouring out, defacing or mixing etc.

Nevertheless, the damage still had to be caused directly by means of a positive act, *corpore datum*. The *praetor*, however, allowed praetorian *actiones in factum* or *utiles legis Aquiliae* where damage was effected by an indirect act. A person's omission did not give rise to an action in delict in classical law.

Justinian allowed an *actio in factum* or *utilis legis Aquiliae*, in case of an omission, but only in cases where the defendant had previously made a positive undertaking and then failed to carry it out completely.

In post-classical law, an *actio utilis legis Aquiliae* was granted for damage resulting from wounding a free person. This was an important exception to the *damnum corpori*-principle, i.e. that a tangible thing had to be damaged. The human body is not a thing, nevertheless, the *paterfamilias* or the injured party himself could claim for the damage which resulted from the wounding. Justinian allowed an *actio in factom legis Aquiliae* when patrimonial loss was caused without physical damage to property. Cf Inst 4 3 16 *sed si non corpore damnum fuerit datum neque corpus laesum fuerit, sed alio modo damnum alicui contigit . . . placuit eum qui obnoxius fuerit in factum actione teneri*, but if the damage was not caused by a direct positive act and no property was physically damaged, but loss had struck someone in a different way . . . in that case the wrongdoer can be held liable with the *actio in factum*. This was the second, most important exception to the *damnum corpori* requirement.

The scope of the *Lex Aquilia* was thus extended beyond the field of physical damage to corporeal property and a foundation was laid for an action for damages in all cases of patrimonial loss.

CULPA

Dolus or *culpa*, intent or negligence, became a requirement for liability *ex lege Aquilia*. Although the Act itself only required that the damage caused had to be done *iniuria*, unlawfully, the lawyers began to interpret *iniuria* in a wider sense, in that an act would only be *iniuria* (i.e. contrary to law) if the act was wrongful and intentional or negligent.

This development was made necessary by the extension of the causal link from direct causation to indirect causation. Consequently, the *mens rea* element developed seperately and was interpolated liberally during the post-classical period. The expression *culpa levissima* was used in this context and denoted a degree of extreme care.

ASSESSMENT OF DAMAGES

According to the first chapter, provision was made for the wrongdoer to pay an amount of money equal to the highest value in the past year, to the owner and chapter 3 provided for an amount equal to the highest value in the past 30 days. These amounts were calculated with regard to the market value of the object in question.

The lawyers assessed the amount by taking *lucrum cessans*, loss of profit, and *damnum emergens*, consequential damages, into account. Thus, the actual loss suffered by the victim became redressible. *Affectiones*, sentimental value, was not taken into account.

The plaintiff made an estimate of his damages and instituted his claim. If the defendant acknowledged his liability, but queried the assessment of damages, a case followed in order to decide on the damages.

If the defendant denied liability and defended the claim, a case followed and if judgment was given against him, he was ordered to pay double the amount of the claim. *Lis crescit infitiando in duplum*, the case increases to double against the defendant who denies. This point illustrated the punitive nature of the *actio legis Aquiliae*. Where more than one person committed *damnum iniuria datum*, the liability was cumulative, i.e. each wrongdoer had to pay the full amount, because an *actio mixta* had a punitive nature.

WHO COULD INSTITUTE THE ACTIO LEGIS AQUILIAE?

The *Lex Aquilia* only granted the action to the owner. It was, therefore, a praetorian extension by the grant of *actiones in factum or utiles legis Aquiliae*, to other interested parties who had suffered financial loss, e.g. the *bona fide possessor*, pledgee, usufructuary, usuary and lessee.

52. Iniuria

Iniuria, injury to the personality, was harmful to the body, honour or reputation of a free person.

The Twelve Tables made provision for various delicts concerning injury to the personality and laid down fixed monetary penalties. The *praetor* introduced the *actio aestimatoria iniuriarum*, because these penalties became ludicrous as the result of inflation. This was an *actio poenalis*, a penal action aimed at punishing the wrongdoer and thus providing amends to the victim. The aggrieved party made an assessment of the amount of the penalty and the instruction to the judge was to decide on an amount *ex aequo et bono*, according to what he thought was just and equitable.

WHO COULD INSTITUTE THE ACTIO INIURIARUM?
The aggrieved person. It was possible to injure a person directly and indirectly; in the last event the injury was against a person *in potestate*, wife, children, slaves, but was in reality aimed at the *paterfamilias* or *dominus*.

AGAINST WHOM COULD THE ACTIO INIURIARUM BE INSTITUTED?
The wrongdoer, his accomplices and accessories were liable and since there was question of an *actio poenalis* their liability was cumulative, i.e. each person had to pay the full penalty.

The action had to be brought within a year.

ELEMENTS OF INIURIA
The first requirement was *contumelia*, any form of affront, i.e. physical injury or insult.

A further element was that the *contumelia* had to be intentional, i.e. *animus iniuriandi*.

Finally, the *contumelia* had to be unlawful in the sense that there was no recognized defence.

Examples of *iniuria* were, preventing somebody to fish in the sea, preventing someone to use a public washing place or to take a seat in a theater, to summon someone *vexandi causa* before a magistrate, to threaten, to announce unjustly that someone owes you a debt, to cause nuisance with smoke, to throw rubbish on your neighbour property, assault and battery, defamation, trespass, exercise of a servitude without a claim of right, public abuse against another, imputation on chastity, thus, any form of insult that human ingenuity can devise.

53. Quasi delicts

Quasi delictum is a wrongful act which creates an obligation between the victim of the wrong and the wrongdoer.

Justinian mentions the following quasi delicts:

IUDEX QUI LITEM SUAM FECIT
A judge who gave a wrong judgment either deliberately or negligently could be sued by the aggrieved litigant with a praetorian action for damages.

RES DEIECTAE VEL EFFUSAE
The occupier of a building from which things were thrown or poured into the

public road, could be sued by passers-by who suffered damage to person or property, with a praetorian action for double the damage.

RES SUSPENSAE VEL POSITAE
The occupier of premises incurred liability when something was suspended, or placed in such a way as to be a danger to passers-by. The amount claimed was a penalty.

ACTIO ADVERSUS EXERCITORES NAVIS AUT CAUPONAE AUT STABULI
The master of a ship, innkeeper and stablekeeper were liable for theft of and damage to the property of their clients committed by their employees. A praetorian action lay for twofold the loss or damage.

54. Praetorian delicts

Although the *praetor* intervened considerably and gave actions with regard to *furtum, rapina, damnum iniuria datum* and *iniuria*, those delicts were considered the delicts of the *ius civile*, since they originated there and the praetorian intervention was only aimed at extending and/or improving redress.

However, the *praetor* went further and introduced new, original actions in respect of some conduct for which the *ius civile* made no provision. The cases for which such actions were introduced were consequently styled praetorian delicts.

There were numerous praetorian delicts, but the most important were *metus*, duress, and *dolus*, fraud.

55. Metus

Metus, duress, consisted in the use of force or the threat of force as a result of which a reasonable person would fear danger to his person, property or his family.

In the old *ius civile* it was irrelevant whether a person was induced by duress to enter into a legal transaction; in other words the transaction was perfectly valid. At an early stage the *praetor* intervened by granting the *exceptio metus causa* where a defendant was forced into concluding a contract from the *ius civile* by means of duress. When the transaction had been executed and the patrimonial loss had been suffered already, the *praetor* made *restitutio in integrum*, restoration of the *status quo*, available to the victim of duress. This remedy was replaced by the *actio quod metus causa*, an *actio mixta* towards the end of the republican period and *metus* thus became a delict.

The *actio metus causa* was applicable whenever somebody suffered financial loss as the result of duress and lay for four times the loss. The action had to be instituted within a year, after which the action lay for the loss. The action contained a *clausula arbitraria*, i.e. the defendant was given the option to restore the thing and be absolved or *nisi restituetur*, if the thing were not restored, to be sentenced to fourfold the value.

WHO COULD INSTITUTE THE ACTIO QUOD METUS CAUSA?
The party who through duress had entered into a legal transaction by which patrimonial loss had been suffered.

AGAINST WHOM COULD THE ACTIO QUOD METUS CAUSA BE INSTITUTED?
Against the person who put pressure on the plaintiff, as well as against any third person who had received benefit from the transaction, even if this person was *bona fide*.

56. Dolus

Dolus, fraud, any guile, chicanery or trick used to circumvent, defraud or dupe another person.

According to the old *ius civile* it was irrelevant whether a person was induced by fraud to enter into a legal transaction; in other words the transaction was perfectly valid.

At the end of the republican era the *praetor* granted the *exceptio doli* where a defendant was conned into concluding a contract from the *ius civile*. If the transaction had been executed and the patrimonial loss had already been suffered, the *praetor* made the *actio doli* available and thus *dolus* became a delict. The *actio doli* was applicable whenever somebody suffered financial loss as the result of fraud and lay for redress for the actual loss suffered.

This means that the *actio doli* was an *actio rei persecutoria*. The action had to be instituted within a year and contained a *clausula arbitraria*. Moreover, the *actio doli* could only be used if no other action was available and was thus a subsidiary action rarely used.

WHO COULD INSTITUTE THE ACTIO DOLI?
The party who as a result of fraud had entered into a legal transaction by which patrimonial loss had been suffered.

AGAINST WHOM COULD THE ACTIO DOLI BE INSTITUTED?
Against the actual fraudulent person. *Condemnatio* entailed *infamia*.

57. Actiones noxales

The *paterfamilias* was held liable for delicts committed by the *alieni iuris* persons in his *potestas*; the owner if a slave was held liable for delicts committed by his slave and under certain circumstances the owner of an animal, could be held liable for damage caused by his animal.

The victim could institute the action which arose from the delict committed by the family member or slave, against the head of the family or owner, in the form of an *actio noxalis*, for example the *actio furti noxalis* was instituted against the owner if his slave had committed theft.

Noxa caput sequitur, liability follows the individual, whereby is meant that the *actio noxalis* had to be instituted against the person who was *pater* or owner of the wrongdoer at the time of *litiscontestatio*, (the joinder of issue) even if another had been *pater* or owner of the wrongdoer at the time of the delict. If the slave had been freed or the *alieni iuris* person emancipated before *litiscontestatio*, they themselves were liable.

When an *actio noxalis* was instituted, the *pater* or owner had two alternatives: firstly, he could hand the wrongdoer over to the aggrieved party, the *noxae deditio*. This was a trace of the primitive era of self-help, when the wrongdoer was handed over for revenge. However, the *noxae deditio* was retained in later law to limit the liability of slave-owners to the value of the slave; the noxal surrender of family members disappeared relatively early.

The second alternative open to the *pater* or owner, was to defend the action and in the case of *condemnatio* pay the penalty and/or damages claimed.

A special *actio noxalis* was found in the *actio de pauperie*, the action which in certain circumstances lay against the owner of an animal. When a four-footed animal acted *contra suam naturam*, contrary to its nature, and caused damage in circumstances in which the owner could not be held at fault, the victim could bring the *actio de pauperie* for damages against the owner. The owner had the option to either pay for the damage done or to surrender the animal.

Noxal liability was based on the fact that the defendant was the *paterfamilias* of the *alieni iuris* or the owner of the slave or animal.

58. Termination of obligations

An obligation could be extinguished in various ways.

The principle mode was *solutio*, performance or fulfilment of the duty undertaken.

WHO HAD TO PERFORM?

The debtor or a third person could discharge the obligation by performance, even if the debtor was unaware of it, or had forbidden it. An exception to the rule that anybody could carry out performance on behalf of the debtor, is found in cases where the nature of the obligation is such that only one particular person, i.e. the debtor can duly perform.

TO WHOM DID PERFORMANCE HAVE TO BE MADE?

To the creditor or to a third person indicated by the creditor, for example a creditor of the creditor.

WHAT HAD TO BE PERFORMED?

The performance had to be that which was due. If the debtor tendered performance of something different, the creditor was entitled to reject this. The creditor could, however, accept the substituted performance and the debtor was thus discharged by *in solutum datio*, i.e. performance of something different from what was due with the agreement of the creditor.

Performance had to be tendered in full, i.e. the creditor could refuse the offer to perform in instalments.

TIME AND PLACE

Where the parties had determined the time at which and the place where performance had to be made in the contract, there was no problem, but where the parties had neglected to do so, these points had to be decided, depending on the circumstances of each case. See also *mora*.

RELEASE

Release takes place when the parties to an obligation agree that the debtor does not have to perform.

The mode of release recognized by the ius civile was the formal *acceptilatio*, the *contrarius actus* (i.e. the act with the contrary effect) of the *stipulatio*. Cf the *acceptilatio, 'Habesne acceptum? Habeo'* and the *stipulatio, '. . . spondesne? Spondeo'*. This meant that only obligations *ex stipulatione* could be released by way of *acceptilatio*. At a later stage, however, all obligations could be released by way of a *pactum de non petendo*, an informal agreement effecting release. In the case of an *obligatio stricti iuris* released by *pactum de non petendo*, the *exceptio pacti conventi* was allowed by the *praetor* if the creditor claimed performance in spite of the *pactum*. In the case of an *obligatio bonae fidei* the *exceptio* was not necessary, because the *bona fides* did not require performance in such a case.

A distinction must be made between the case where the debtor from a consensual contract was released from his obligation by way of a *pactum de non petendo* and the case where the whole consensual contract was revoked. The last possibility only existed *re integra*, i.e. if nothing of the contract had been executed yet.

COMPENSATION

Compensatio, compensation or set-off takes place when two people are both debtor and creditor to each other. Under certain circumstances both debts are discharged, if they were equal; if unequal, the smaller is discharged, the larger remaining in force for the balance. Classical Roman law did not recognize *compensatio* except in a few exceptional cases. Justinian generally allowed compensation by providing that reciprocal debts were *ipso iure*, automatically, totally or partially discharged, if the debts were of the same nature and fully due.

MERGER

Confusio, merger takes place when the capacities of creditor and debtor of the same obligation are combined in the same person. The consequence of merger is that the debt is *ipso iure*, automatically, discharged.

NOVATION

Novatio, novation, is the termination of an obligation by its replacement with another.

Novatio was originally effected by means of *stipulatio* but could in later law take place by means of an informal agreement, *pactum*.

Novatio was important in Roman law, since in this manner any existing obligation could be transformed into an obligation *ex stipulatione*. Moreover, one of the parties to an existing obligation could be replaced by another, by way of novation, which was an important factor in view of the intensely personal nature of obligations and the consequential non-transmissibility.

REQUIREMENTS FOR NOVATIO

Firstly, there had to be an existing obligation. The performance due under the new obligation had to be the same as under the original obligation, *idem debitum*. Nevertheless, *aliquid novi*, something new, had to be present in the new obligation as well, for example, change of parties, introduction or removal of a condition or a term, or a new form of contract, namely, a *stipulatio*. Finally, there had to be *animus novandi*, the intention to novate.

EFFECTS OF NOVATIO

The original obligation was terminated *ipso iure*. All *accessoria* (accessories to it), such as interest, suretyships and pledges, were also discharged.

Delegatio, delegation, is novation whereby the parties to an obligation, either creditor or debtor are changed.

Cession, i.e. the transfer of a personal right to another, in such manner that the person to whom the cession is made, the cessionary, takes the place of the creditor, was not recognized by Roman law, in view of the personal nature of legal transactions.

The same result could, however, be attained by making use of *delegatio*, but *delegatio* should not be mistaken for cession. In the case of cession a personal right is transferred, while in the case of delegation an existing obligation is terminated and replaced with another.

FURTHER METHODS BY WHICH OBLIGATIONS ARE DISCHARGED

Transactio, compromise, is an agreement whereby the parties settle a dispute between them. If the dispute related to an obligation, this obligation was discharged by compromise.

Litiscontestatio, supervening impossibility without blame, resolutive conditions and terms and in some cases death of one of the parties, or the lapse of time, could also discharge obligations.

CHAPTER V – The law of persons

The Roman law of persons, *ius quod ad personas pertinet*, denotes that part of the law concerned with the *status hominum*, the legal position of the human being. This implies that the Roman law of persons busied itself only with natural persons, irrespective of whether these persons were the subject or the object of rights. Roman law of persons covered the *status libertatis*, free or slave, *status civitatis*, Roman citizen or not, *status familiae*, dependent or independent, as well as other factors such as age, sex or mental state which had relevance with regard to a human being's legal position. The Roman law of persons has little importance in modern law.

1. What is a persona

Persona included every human being, hence even slaves were persons and therefore, treated under the law of persons.

In modern legal systems, the term 'person' denotes the subject of rights and duties and thus apart from human or natural persons the so-called juristic person is also recognized.

Although Roman law also knew and recognized non-human subjects of rights and duties, municipalities, private bodies, the state and the like, these were not considered *personae* and fell outside the scope of the law of persons.

A *persona* originated at birth and terminated on death. In certain circumstances the unborn child was regarded as already born. This is known as the *nasciturus* fiction.

2. Status libertatis; slavery

All men were either free or slaves. Slavery was very important in Rome, but is only of historical interest today.

Slavery arose with birth from a slave woman, capture or punishment and ended with the death of a slave or *manumissio iusta ac legitima*, a formally correct way of granting a slave freedom.

Freedmen, *libertini* or *liberti*, became Roman citizens. There were informal ways of freeing a slave which created many problems. A slave was not the subject of rights and duties, but the objects of rights and duties. A slave had, however, a limited legal capacity, that is a capacity to do legal acts. He could not execute all legal acts. For example, a slave could not marry and had no standing in the courts, but he could enter into some legal acts, for example a contract. These legal acts had, however, special legal consequences; anything acquired by a slave, accrued to his master, but he could not impose duties on himself nor on his master. This position was made workable by the *peculium* and the *actiones adiecticiae qualitatis*, which institutions introduced the concepts of limited liability and agency into Roman law.

When a slave committed a delict, an *actio noxalis* could be brought against his master. A change of status was *capitis deminutio* and *capitis deminutio maxima* involved loss of liberty.

3. Status civitatis

Civitas Romana, Roman citizenship, was a privilege, which was usually acquired by means of conception during a Roman marriage or birth from an unmarried Roman mother. Furthermore, citizenship could be acquired by a *iusta ac legitima manumissio* and by the granting of citizenship by law, or decree by the authorities. Towards the end of republic citizenship was granted to all inhabitants of Italy and in 212 AD the emperor Caracalla granted by the *constitutio Antoniniana*, Roman citizenship to virtually all inhabitants of the empire.

Capitis deminutio media or *minor* denoted the loss of citizenship.

The freeborn Roman citizen had the following rights, depending on age, sex and mental capacity. In public law he had the right to vote in the assemblies, the *ius suffragii*, and the right to stand for public office, the *ius honorum*, as well as the right to serve in the Roman legions.

In private law he had the right to enter into a marriage according to Roman law, the *ius conubii*; he had standing in the courts and the right to take part in Roman law, the *ius commercii*.

4. Status familiae

The *status familiae* was the factor which decided the question whether a person was *sui iuris*, independent, or *alieni iuris*, subject to another. The *alieni iuris* persons were under the authority of the *paterfamiliaes*, the oldest male member of the family. The *paterfamilias* was the central figure in the law of persons. His authority, *patria potestas* over the members of his family, *manus* over his wife, was the tie that bound the members of his family together. Thus, *familia* denoted all persons under the authority of the same *paterfamilias*. The relationship between the members of a family in Roman law was *agnatio*, the tie which related the members of a *familia*, because they fell under the *potestas* of the same *pater*.

Blood relationship was irrelevant and was only gradually recognized by the Roman law of succession.

Originally, the power of the head of the family over his dependants was absolute. He had the *ius vitae necisque*, the power of life and death; he had the power to sell his children; he could marry them off, give them in adoption or emancipate them. Finally, the *alieni iuris* persons were financially completely dependant on him, since they had no proprietary capacity.

The absolute powers of the *paterfamilias* over his dependants were no different from the powers an owner had over his slaves and were consistent with the primitive origin of Rome, where there was one lord and master on the farm. As Roman society developed a steady reduction of the powers of the *pater* appeared; the *ius vitae necisque* was abolished together with the power to sell children and gradually duties were placed on the *pater* with regard to his *alieni iuris*, for example, the duty of support, the duty to give his daughters a dowry etc.

5. Members of the familia

The members of a *familia* were those people who were in the *potestas* of the same *pater*, i.e. the *alieni iuris* persons.

The following members of a *familia* could be distinguished. Firstly, the children from the Roman marriage of the *paterfamilias*. *Pater est quem nuptiae demonstrant*, the marriage indicates who the father is. This rebuttable presumption indicated, in classical law, that children conceived during a marriage were considered the legitimate children of the husband, i.e. were in his *potestas*. Justinian decreed that children conceived or born during a marriage were presumed to be the legitimate children of the husband.

Secondly, the grandchildren and further descendants from marriages of sons *in potestate*, i.e. in the power of the *paterfamilias*, were members of the *familia*, i.e. were in the *potestas* of the *paterfamilias*. Illegitimate children were at all times *sui iuris* at birth.

If the marriage was *cum manu*, with marital power, the wife was a member of her husband's *familia* where she stood in the position of a daughter, *filiae loco*, in regard to her husband. If the marriage was *sine manu*, without marital power, she remained under the power of her own *paterfamilias*, or *sui iuris*. Daughters-in-law who were married *cum manu* with sons *in potestate* were also in the *potestas* of the *paterfamilias*.

Finally, legitimated, adopted and adrogated children were part of the *familia*. From this it has become clear that the power of the *pater* over the members of his *familia* arose by descent, namely conception or birth during a

Roman marriage; a marriage *cum manu*, legitimation and adoption, or adrogation.

6. Legitimation

Legitimatio, legitimation, was one of the institutions whereby some illegitimate children could acquire the status of legitimacy. In Roman law this meant that the child in question was brought *in potestate*.

CLASSES OF ILLEGITIMATE CHILDREN

There were three classes of illegitimate children.

Liberi naturales, children born out of a concubinate; *spurii* or *vulgo concepti*, children born out of extramarital affairs; *adulterini et incestuosi*, children born from adulterine and incestuous relationships.

Concubinatus, concubinage, developed during the post-classical era into a durable monogamous cohabitation between a man and a woman. This showed a great resemblance with marriage and was eventually considered a type of secondrate marriage. Legislation was enacted which introduced the possibility of legitimising the offspring of a concubinage, by way of transforming this relationship into a marriage.

LEGITIMATIO PER SUBSEQUENS MATRIMONIUM

Justinian finally regulated this method of legitimation. Only *liberi naturales* could be legitimated by this method.

Instrumenta dotalia, a document regulating marriage settlements, was required as proof that the concubinage was indeed transformed into a marriage. Furthermore, the parties should not have been prohibited to marry each other at the time of the conception of the children and finally, the children themselves had to consent, if possible.

As a result of the marriage, the children would fall into the *potestas* of their father.

Justinian also created another form of legitimation, *legitimatio per rescriptum principis*, legitimation by a rescript of the emperor. In cases where a marriage between the concubinaries was impossible, a father might petition the emperor or enter such a request in his will, for a rescript legitimating his children by a concubine, who was either dead or unfit to marry.

In this case it was a condition that the father had no legitimate issue and that the children in question assented, if possible. The *rescriptum principis*, rescript of the emperor, declared the child in *potestate* of the father.

A third form of legitimation, *legitimatio per oblationem curiae* was introduced during the late empire, allowing *liberi naturales* to be made legitimate by enrolment as a member of the *curia*, the municipal council.

7. Adoption

Adoption was one of the institutions whereby a person could be brought *in potestate*. Adoption was an important institution for the Romans in view of their concern for the continuation of the *familia*, family name and cult of their ancestors. When the fear arose that a *familia* might become extinct, an outsider was brought *in potestate* by means of adoption and thus became a member of the *familia*.

Roman law knew two separate forms of adoption, i.e. *adrogatio*, the adoption of a *sui iuris* person, and *adoptio*, the adoption of an *alieni iuris* person. *Adrogatio* took place when a *sui iuris* was brought *in potestate*. This was an important event, involving the extinction of one *familia* to perpetuate another. Not only the adrogated person, but all *alieni iuris* persons in his power and his property came in the *potestas* of the *pater adrogans*. Consequently in ancient Roman law the people had to approve an *adrogatio* and the matter thus went to the *comitia*. Since *adrogatio* took place in the *comitia*, women and persons under the age of puberty could not be adrogated. In the later empire *adrogatio* was performed *per rescriptum principis*, by imperial rescript. Justinian required the *pater adrogans* to be over sixty or unlikely to have children; no one could adrogate if he had children already and the *pater adrogans* had to be at least eighteen years older than the adrogated person. Furthermore, there were special safeguards in respect of the *adrogatio* of *impuberes, sui iuris* persons under the age of puberty.

Adoptio took place when an *alieni iuris* person was transferred from the *potestas* of one *pater* into the *potestas* of another.

Originally *adoptio* was not possible in Roman law, but interpretation of a provision of the Twelve Tables *'si pater filium ter venum dicit, filius a patre liber esto'*, if a father sells his son three times, the son will be free from his father, introduced the possibility of *adoptio*.

The provision was meant to keep *patres*, who regularly exercised their right to sell their children, in check, but interpretation employed this rule to achieve *adoptio*. The original *paterfamilias* sold his son three times by way of *mancipatio* to the adoptive *pater*, who immediately freed the son twice, whereupon the *filius* reverted to his father's *potestas*. After the third *mancipatio* the son was remancipated to his original *pater*. The adopting *pater* instituted procedings claiming the *filius* to be his son. The former *pater* offered no defence and the *praetor* addicted the *filius* to the adopting *pater*. The first stage broke the existing *potestas* and the second stage transferred the *potestas* by *in iure cessio*. Only son's had to be sold thrice and where other *alieni iuris* persons were given in adoption, a single sale by *mancipatio* sufficed.

Justinian considerably altered *adoptio*. He provided that both *patres* and the *alieni iuris* in question should appear before a magistrate, where the existing *pater* should make a declaration and the other parties should give their agreement. The magistrate recorded the facts.

Justinian provided, furthermore, that only an ascendant could adopt with full effect, i.e. that the *alieni iuris* left the *potestas* of his existing *pater* and fell under the *potestas* of the adopting *pater*, his ascendant, in practice his grandfather. This was *adoptio plena*. All other adoption was *adoptio minus plena* and the *potestas* did not pass. The *alieni iuris* remained in the *potestas* of his original *pater*, but acquired the right of intestate succession to the person who adopted him. The same requirements as in the case of *adrogatio* were applicable, since the principle *adoptio naturam imitatur*, adoption adhered to the rules of nature, was followed.

8. Capacity of filiusfamilias to enter into legal acts

Originally the *potestas* of a *pater* over his children was ended, only by the death of either *pater* or child. Thus the adult *filius* remained in the *potestas* of his *pater*.

When of full age, the *filius* had, in public law, the right to vote, to stand for office and to serve in the legions, but in private law he remained subject to his father's *potestas*, which affected primarily his proprietary capacity. Any acquisition by a *filius* vested in his *pater*, with the result that the *filius* never obtained property of his own.

At puberty the *filius* acquired capacity to enter into legal acts, but these acts had the same consequences as transactions entered into by slaves, i.e. transactions whereby something was acquired, had the effect that acquisition accrued to the *pater*; transactions whereby an obligation was undertaken did not bind the *pater*. Although these obligations bound the *filius* himself, this meant nothing practically, because execution against his estate was impossible and execution against his person was considered contrary to the *patriapotestas*.

Two institutions, the *peculium* and the *actiones adiecticiae qualitatis*, made the position of the *filius* acceptable in everyday life.

A *peculium* was property placed by the master or *pater* under control of a slave or *filius* respectively. This remained the property of the master or *pater*, but the slave and *filius* could for all practical purposes deal on equal terms with third parties. This type of *peculium* was the so-called *peculium profecticium*.

The *actiones adiecticiae qualitalis* were actions by which a third party who had entered into a legal act with a slave or *filius* could sue the master or *paterfamilias*. Thus, in certain cases agency imposing liability on the principal by a slave or *filius* was recognized. See *supra* part IV, 18 and 19.

Furthermore, during the empire certain exceptions to the proprietary incapacity of the *filius* were introduced. During the reign of Augustus the *peculium castrense* appeared, comprising everything the *filius* acquired in respect of his military service and gradually this *peculium castrense* was regarded as the property of the *filius*.

In post-classical law the same principle was extended to everything the *filius* acquired from other professions, such as a civil servant, priest and certain other professions, the *peculium quasi-castrense*. Finally, the *peculium adventicium* was introduced comprising the inheritance from the *filius'* mother, the *bona materna*, and eventually extending to any acquisitions other than those from the *pater*. This *peculium* gradually became regarded as the property of the *filius*, but the *pater* had a *usufruct* over it. The end result was thus, that in the Justinian law any acquisition by a *filius* vested in him with the exception of the *peculium profecticium*, while the father had *usufruct* over the *peculium adventicium*.

9. Termination of patriapotestas

The *patriapotestas* was ended by the death of a *pater* or *alieni iuris, capitis deminutio* of a *pater* or *alieni iuris, adoptio, marriage cum manu* of a daughter and *emancipatio. Emancipatio* took place when the *pater* released an *alieni iuris* person from his *potestas*. The same rule from the Twelve Tables which made possible *adoptio*, was used to introduce emancipation.

The father sold the *filius* three times by way of *mancipatio* to a trusted person and the latter freed the *filius* each time. Only sons had to be sold thrice, while one sale sufficed for other *alieni iuris* persons.

Justinian replaced the old procedure with a declaration by the *pater* before an official, while the consent of the *alieni iuris* was also required.

10. Marriage

An attempt to define marriage is pointless, since this institution underwent drastic changes through the ages. Confer the definition by Modestinus which is found at the beginning of the title on marriage in the Digest: *'Nuptiae sunt coniunctio maris et feminae et consortium omnis vitae, divini et humani iuris communicatio'* marriage is the union of a man and a woman and a community for life, a fusion of divine and human law. The community for life referred to, might have been applicable with regard to the marriage *cum manu* in ancient times, as well as the Christian marriage in the post-classical empire, but did definitely not apply to the marriage of later republican and classical times. These marriages constituted a loose band, easily entered into and just as easily terminated.

Marriage founded the *familia*, which was the foundation of Roman society.

Most marriages followed on an engagement, *sponsalia*. Originally, marriages were arranged by the respective *patresfamilias* by means of *sponsio*, a formal verbal contract, which was enforceable by action. In later law the engagement rested only on agreement of the parties, although the consent of the *patres* was required. Breach of promise was no longer actionable, but regained certain legal consequences in post-classical law, i.e. forfeiting twofold of the *arra sponsalis*, the engagement gift ordinarily consisting of an amount of money, if the betrothal was terminated without mutual consent or without good cause. Usually the marriage followed shortly on the engagement.

PREREQUISITES FOR A VALID MARRIAGE

Firstly, both parties were to have the *ius conubii*, the capacity to contract a Roman marriage.

Secondly, both parties had to be above the age of puberty, the ages being fourteen for boys and twelve for girls.

If the parties were *alieni iuris*, the consent of the *patresfamilias* was also necessary. The *pater* could withhold consent for reasonable cause, but otherwise provision was made for the granting of consent by a magistrate.

Finally, there were to be no impediments. The most important impediments were based on relationship by blood, marriage and adoption.

Adscendentes, ascendants, and *descendentes*, descendants, in the direct line could never marry each other. This prohibition was applicable irrespective of whether the relationship in question rested on *cognatio*, blood relationship, *agnatio*, the relationship between members of a *familia* based on the fact that they were in the power of the same *paterfamilias*, as well as *adfinitas*, the relationship by marriage.

Furthermore, *collaterales*, collaterals could not marry each other, if they were too closely related, but the forbidden degrees varies through the ages. This prohibition applied to *cognatio, agnatio* and *adfinitas* relationship.

If a marriage was contracted contrary to these prohibitions, the crime of *incestus* was committed. The marriage was null and void, children born from such a relationship were *incestuosi* and both parties were punished.

There were also prohibitions on the intermarriage of certain persons by reason of morality or public policy. These impediments underwent drastic changes through the ages.

Difference in class or rank formed an important impediment; soldiers on service were not allowed to marry; a guardian was not allowed to marry his ward; provincial officials were not allowed to marry a woman of the province; adulterers could not marry each other.

If a marriage was contracted contrary to any of these prohibitions, the marriage was null and void, the children *spurii* and the parties not punished.

A further impediment was only applicable to women. Originally, a widow had to observe a lapse of ten months after the death of her husband before remarrying. This *tempus lugendi*. period of mourning, had a sacral origin. In the fourth century AD imperial legislation extended the period to one year, the *annus luctus*. Moreover, the *annus luctus* had acquired juridical significance, namely, to prevent *turbatio* or *confusio sanguinis*, doubt about the paternity, which a hasty remarriage might create in view of the presumption concerning paternity. Thus, the *annus luctus* was extended to cases where the marriage was dissolved by divorce.

A marriage within the *annus luctus* was, however, valid, but the woman was punished with *infamia*.

Augustus enacted legislation in an attempt to stabilize and promote marriage and procreation, as well as to restore moral rectitude. However, this legislation did not achieve its goals and its provisions did not obtain efficacy.

CONCLUSION OF MARRIAGE

Consensus facit nuptias, agreement creates a marriage. This means that for the creation of a valid marriage nothing more was necessary than the agreement between the parties to be married, i.e. to enter a durable monogamous cohabitation aimed at the procreation of children. The *affectio maritalis*, the intent to be married, distinguished the marriage from a concubinage. No formalities were required for the conclusion of a marriage.

The *affectio maritalis* could be deduced from the *deductio in domum mariti*, the marriage ceremony, or from the fact that an *instrumentum dotale* was drawn up. Nevertheless, these were never requirements for the conclusion of a marriage.

11. Marriage cum manu and sine manu

The conclusion of a marriage should be distinguished from the *conventio in manum*, the passage of the wife into the power of her husband or her husband's *pater*. The Roman's original attitude was that every marriage should be *cum manu*, but during the republic the *sine manu* marriage made its appearance and the final result was that the *cum manu* marriage disappeared completely. *Manus*, the power of the husband or his *pater* over the wife, could be created by *confarreatio*, a religious ceremony, *coemptio*, a conveyance by *mancipatio*, and *usus*, lapse of time of one year.

THE LEGAL EFFECTS OF THE CUM MANU MARRIAGE

The woman passed into the power of her husband or, if he was himself *in potestate*, into the power of his *pater*. This implies, that if she had been *sui iuris* she became *alieni iuris* and her property transferred to her husband or his *pater*. Everything she acquired subsequently accrued immediately to her husband or his *pater*, with the result that she never had property of her own. If she had been *filiafamilias* before her marriage, i.e. *in potestate* of her *pater*, she left her original *familia* and became a member of her husband's *familia*. The wife was *filiae loco*, in the position of a daughter in her husband's *familia*.

THE LEGAL EFFECTS OF THE SINE MANU MARRIAGE

The wife did not fall under the power of her husband or his *pater*. If she had been *sui iuris* before her marriage, she remained *sui iuris* and retained her own property. Everything she acquired subsequently, accrued to her own property. She was not a member of her husband's *familia*. If she had been *filiafamilias* before her marriage, she remained in the *potestas* of her *pater* and remained a member of her original *familia*.

Thus the legal effects of the *sine manu* marriage were few. The marriage partners stood legally in the same position as strangers to each other, but in later law certain legal consequences were coupled to the fact that they were married to one another. They could not institute infaming actions against each other; a *donatio inter virum et uxorem*, a donation between husband and wife, was prohibited; *intercessio*, intercession, by the wife for her husband was null and void.

12. Dissolution of marriage

A marriage would be dissolved by the death, enslavement or loss of citizenship of either party; it would also be ended by divorce, which was the commonest form of terminating a marriage. Since a marriage was informally contracted by *consensus*, it could be informally ended by *dissensus*, the lack of *consensus*. This means that a marriage was dissolved if one or both parties did not want to be married anymore and terminated the cohabitation. Just as no formalities were required for the conclusion of a marriage, no formalities were required for a divorce. To provide certainty whether a divorce had taken place or not, it was customary to send a *libellus repudii*, a letter of separation, although this was not required for a divorce.

Where the marriage had been *cum manu*, the *manus* over the wife had to be terminated when the parties divorced. This was done by a *contrarius actus*, a reverse act, namely *diffareatio* or *remancipatio*.

The Christian emperors disapproved of unmotivated onesided dissolutions of marriage and penalized the party financially who divorced in this manner, but the marriage was still dissolved. Good causes motivating divorce were adultery, promiscuous behaviour, abuse, attempt on life etc.

Thus, the *divortium ex iusta causa*, divorce for good cause, came to be distinguished from the *divortium sine ulla causa*, divorce without cause. In the first instance the guilty party suffered financial penalties, while in latter the repudiating party was penalized financially.

13. Marriage settlements: dos and donatio propter nuptias

It was a general usage, a moral duty and eventually a legal duty for the father to give the husband a *dos*, a dowry, on the marriage of his daughter. As a rule it was the father of the bride who gave the dowry, but it could be the bride herself or another member of her family or even an outsider who provided the dowry.

The primary function of the dowry was *ad onera matrimonii sustinenda*, to contribute to the expenses of a marriage. In addition it came to provide for the wife after the termination of the marriage. It thus follows, that, although the *dos* became the property of the husband, the whole dowry or part of it had to be returned on termination of the marriage.

The *dos* could consist of any form of property, corporeal or incorporeal, movable or immovable. Dowry could be constituted by any legal act which enlarged the estate of the husband: *dotis datio*, transfer of the *dos, dotis dictio* or *dotis promissio*, enforceable promise of the dowry.

The husband became the owner of the *dos*, but gradually his rights over it were increasingly restricted and in Justinian law his ownership of the *dos* had become purely formal and his position was in reality that of a usufructuary. Originally there was no legal duty on the husband to return the *dos* on termination of the marriage, but with the increasing popularity of divorce the wife acquired a right to her *dos*.

THE DUTY TO RETURN THE DOS

In many instances the return of the *dos* was guaranteed by *stipulatio* between the husband and the provider of the *dos*, in which case the provider could claim with the appropriate action arising from the *stipulatio*.

In the absence of a *stipulatio* to this effect there was no legal duty to return the *dos*. However, before the end of the republic the *praetor* granted the *actio rei uxoriae*, whereby the wife, or in some instances her *pater*, could obtain the return of the *dos* or a portion of it, on the termination of the marriage. Since this action was based on good faith the judge could take the circumstances of the particular case into consideration and consequently a number of *retentiones ex dote*, deductions from the dowry, developed in practice. These were the *retentio propter mores*, a deduction where the woman had been guilty of immorality, *retentio propter res donatas*, the deduction for gifts during marriage, *retentio propter res amotas*, a deduction for property removed by the wife, *retentio propter liberos*, deduction in respect of children.

Justinian ruled that in all cases of termination of the marriage the wife or her heirs could claim the return of the *dos* from the husband with the *actio dotis* or *actio de dote*. In addition, he gave the wife a privileged tacit hypothec over the property of the husband to secure the return of her dowry. This means that she could with the *actio hypothecaria* or *actio quasi serviana* claim possession of the property of her dowry, and all property which had ever belonged to her husband, from anybody in possession of such property. She could retain the property of the dowry and she could exercise her *ius distrahendi* with regard to the other property to satisfy her claim in respect of that portion of the *dos* which could not be recovered. This implies that in Justinian law the wife had for all practical purposes become the owner of the *dos*.

DONATIO ANTE OR PROPTER NUPTIAS

The later empire saw the development of another institution that derived from the East. This was virtually a counter-dowry given or promised by the husband to his wife before the marriage with the purpose of providing for his wife and children after dissolution of the marriage. Justinian allowed such donations even during the marriage.

14. Guardianship and curatorship; general

In principle the *sui iuris* person was independant, had his own property and was capable to perform legal acts. Certain *sui iuris* persons, however, were on the basis of their immaturity, sex or mental deficiencies not capable of conducting their own affairs. These persons were wholly or partially incapable of performing legal acts and were therefore, placed under *tutela*, guardianship, or *cura* curatorship.

Originally these institutions amounted to a right of the agnatic relations over the *sui iuris* and his estate, which right was of the same nature as the *patriapotestas*. Their initial function was to safeguard the financial interest of the agnatic family rather than to protect the interests of the incapable *sui iuris* person. Thus it was the *proximus agnatus*, the nearest agnatic relative, who was both the intestate heir of the person in question, and the tutor or curator according to the *ius civile*. In developed law these institutions were recognized as existing for the benefit of the incapable *sui iuris* and guardianship and curatorship became a *munus*, a duty without advantages.

Two forms of guardianship existed in Roman law, namely, *tutela impuberum*, guardianship over *impuberes*, persons below the age of puberty, and *tutela mulierum*, guardianship over women. The latter was characteristic of the patriarchal Roman society where a woman always had to be under the power of a male, i.e. the *manus* of her husband, the *potestas* of her father, or, in the case of the *sui iuris* woman, the *tutela*. This form of *tutela* lost any real significance during the early days of the empire.

15. Tutela impuberum

Tutela impuberum, guardianship over *impuberes, sui iuris* persons below the age of puberty, was, however, a different matter. It needs no explanation that these persons were incapable of conducting their own affairs.

In developed law the age of puberty was set at fourteen years for boys and twelve for girls. *Impuberes* could be subdivided into *infantes*, those unable to speak and from 407 AD, those below the age of seven years, and *infanti proximi* and *infantia maiores*, those over the age of seven but below fourteen or twelve years.

VARIOUS TYPES OF TUTELA IMPUBERUM

Tutela testamentaria

Tutela testamentaria was the most usual and important form of *tutela*. Persons below the age of puberty as a rule became *sui iuris* only on the death of their *pater*. *Patres*, who foresaw this eventuality could appoint in their will a *tutor* or *tutores* for the *alieni iuris* persons in their *potestas*, who would become *sui iuris* on his death, but had not yet reached the age of puberty.

Tutela legitima

Tutela legitima arose in the absence of a *tutor testamentarius*. According to the Twelve Tables the *proximus agnatus*, the nearest agnate of the child who was also the intestate heir of the child, became *ipso iure*, automatically, his or her *tutor*. Justinian made the *proximus cognatus*, the nearest cognatic relative also *tutor legitimus*.

Tutela dativa

In the absence of a *tutor testamentarius* or a *tutor legitimus*, the state appointed a *tutor*. In Rome a *tutor* could be appointed by the *praetor* and a majority of the *tribuni plebis*, and in the provinces, by the *praeses provinciae*, the provincial governor. In the later imperial period changes were made in this respect.

WHO COULD BE TUTOR?

Any male Roman citizen above the age of puberty could be *tutor*, but in later law the required age was raised to twenty-five years. When guardianship developed into a *munus*, a public duty, the *tutor* had to accept the office, but in certain instances *excusationes*, pleas for declining appointment, were allowed, for example advanced age, the tenure of certain offices or exercise of certain professions.

FUNCTIONS OF THE TUTOR

In origin it was the duty of the tutor to protect the person as well as the estate of the *impubes*. The nature of the *tutela* was identical to that of the *patria potestas*. This meant that the tutor stood *domini loco*, in the position of an owner, in respect of the ward's estate. In developed law the tutor's task was limited to the protection of the ward's estate, and the care for the person of the *impubes* was in the hands of the mother or other family. The functions of the *tutor* became more specific and his power over the estate became subject to limitations.

The *tutor's* functions varied according to the type of *impubes* he was concerned with.

ADMINISTRATIO

If the ward was *infans* and thus wholly without legal capacity, the *tutor* had the *administratio* of the estate. This means that he administered the ward's affairs and had to commit all transactions in respect of the estate. Since Roman law did not recognize representation all transactions in respect of the estate were entered into by the *tutor* in his own name and had legal effect towards him and not towards the ward. The practical solution to this problem was to use a slave of the estate to enter into legal acts regarding the estate.

AUCTORITATIS INTERPOSITIO

Once the ward was over seven years he had a limited legal capacity. The ward could enter unassisted into legal acts from which he benefitted, but transactions whereby he incurred a burden, could be performed only with the approval of his *tutor*. The *tutor* had to be present and informally assent to the transaction. If the ward entered into a bilateral contract without the *tutor's auctoritas*, the result was that he bound the other party to himself but incurred no legal liability himself. An imperial rescript mitigated the injustice of this, by holding the ward liable to the extent of his enrichment.

POWERS OF THE GUARDIAN IN RESPECT OF THE ESTATE

Originally, the *tutor* was *domini loco* in respect of the estate and could alienate the ward's property. An important limit on the *tutor's* power of alienation was imposed by an *oratio Severi*, a *Senatus Consultum* on instigation of the emperor Severus, around the end of the second century AD, which prohibited the sale of *praedia rustica et suburbana*, agricultural and undeveloped urban land.

Constantine extended the prohibition to all valuable assets of the estate, which could be sold only in case of necessity with magisterial authority.

On the other hand certain obligations were placed upon the *tutor*. He had to make an inventory of the estate at the beginning of his guardianship, and in certain instances had to provide security for the safety of the ward's estate, the so-called *cautio rem pupulli salvam fore*.

REMEDIES AGAINST THE TUTOR

Where the tutor had made the *cautio rem pupilli salvam fore*, he could be held liable with the *actio ex stipulatu* in the event of maladministration.

Moreover, from the time of the Twelve Tables anyone other than the ward himself could lay the *accusatio*, accusation, of the *crimen suspecti tutoris*, the crime of the suspect *tutor*, before the *praetor* or the *praeses provinciae*. If the accusation held good, the *tutor* was removed. The *crimen* was a matter of public law, but in the field of private law the Twelve Tables granted the *actio de rationibus distrahendis*, at the end of the *tutela*, against a *tutor*, who had been guilty of embezzling the estate. This action was delictual and the *tutor* was sentenced *in duplum*, for double the damage suffered. This action could, however, only be instituted against a fraudulent *tutor* and consequently another action appeared, the *actio tutelae*.

This was an *actio bonae fidei* which the ward could bring at the end of the *tutela* against the *tutor*. With this action the ward claimed for any acquisitions made for the estate by the *tutor*, as well as damage suffered as a result of the *dolus* and *culpa levis in concreto* of the *tutor*. It would be possible that the *tutor* had a counterclaim for disbursements made by his own estate and/or damage suffered as a result of the *tutela*. Hence, there was an *actio tutelae contraria* by which the *tutor* could sue the ward. These actions were *quasi ex contractu*.

Finally, the ward could make use of the *actio hypothecaria* or *quasi Serviana*, from the time of Constantine. This emperor created a tacit hypothec on the *tutor's* estate to secure any claims the ward might have against his guardian.

TERMINATION OF TUTELA

Tutela usually ended upon the attainment of puberty by the ward. Other ways were by the death and *capitis deminutio* of ward or guardian, a successful *excusatio* and a successful accusation on the grounds of the *crimen suspecti tutoris*.

16. Curatorship

Curatorship was relevant whenever a *sui iuris* person above the age of puberty was not capable of conducting his own affairs on the grounds of a disability. Since these disabilities varied, a number of curatorships existed, and the functions of the curator were never the same but depended upon the particular disability. The most important forms of *cura* were *cura minorum, cura furiosi* and *cura prodigi*.

CURA MINORUM

Cura minorum was the curatorship over *minores*, who were *sui iuris* persons above the age of puberty but under twenty-five years of age. In principle these *sui iuris* persons had full legal capacity, but twelve and fourteen is obviously rather young to competently manage one's own affairs, with the result that gradually the *cura minorum* developed.

The *lex Plaetoria* of about 200 BC made fraud on a person under twenty-five punishable. The next step was that the *praetor* granted *restitutio in integrum*, restitution of the status *ante quo*, whenever a *minor* had suffered loss as the result of his youthful inexperience. The result of this was that for practical purposes *puberes, sui iuris* persons above the age of puberty, reached full legal capacity only at the age of twenty-five, since third parties refused to enter into important transactions with them in view of the possibility of *restitutio in integrum*. The practice accordingly developed that adults in dealing with a *minor*, required the assistance of a *curator*, which safeguarded them against a possible *restitutio in integrum*. Consequently, a *minor* had to ask the assistance of a *curator* for any important transaction. Towards the end of the classical period the *curator ad hoc* was replaced by a single permanent *curator*. This type of *curator* assimilated increasingly with the *tutor* of an *impubes* and his function in post-classical law became *auctoritatis interpositio*, the interposing of approval in transactions incurring burdens.

The *minor* had the *actio negotiorum gestorum* for claims against the *curator*, while the latter could institute the *actio negotiorum gestorum contraria*. Minority, and thus *cura*, lasted until the age of twenty-five, unless *venia aetatis* was granted.

17. Cura furiosi

Cura furiosi, curatorship over a lunatic, went back to the Twelve Tables where it was provided that a *sui iuris* who went mad passed into the *cura* of his nearest agnate. *Furiosus nullum negotium genere potest, quia non intellegit quid agat*, a lunatic cannot enter into any legal act, since he does not understand what he does.

The *curator* had care of the person as well as the estate of the *furiosus*. The *cura furiosi* came into effect automatically at the manifestation of lunacy and ended automatically when he regained sanity. Where there was no *proximus agnatus* the *praetor* appointed a *curator*.

FUNCTIONS AND POWERS OF THE CURATOR

The functions of the curator were similar to those of the *tutor* over an *infans*, i.e. *administratio*. This means that he administered the lunatic's affairs and had to effect all transactions in respect of the estate. Moreover, he had to take care of the person of the *furiosus*.

The *curator* stood *domini loco* in respect of the estate and could alienate property of the estate. He was liable for maladministration and the *actio negotiorum gestorum directa* and *contraria* were available to enforce the claims between the parties.

18. Cura prodigi

Cura prodigi, curatorship over a prodigal also went back to the Twelve Tables where it was provided that the estate of a prodigal could be placed under the *cura* of the *proximus agnatus. Cura prodigi* had to be applied for and the *praetor* granted an interdict preventing the prodigal the conduct of his affairs and appointing the *proximus agnatus* or, in his default, a third party as *curator*.

The prodigal had limited legal capacity, which could be compared to that of an *impubes* after *infantia*. The prodigal could enter unassisted into legal acts by which he benefitted, but was incapable of transactions whereby a burden was incurred.

THE FUNCTIONS AND POWERS OF THE CURATOR

The *curator* had to administer the estate of the prodigal and had to perform all transactions whereby detriment was incurred. The *curator* probably stood *domini loco* in respect of the estate of the prodigal, and rights and duties were enforced by the *actio negotiorum gestorum directa* and *contraria* respectively.

CHAPTER VI – The law of succession

The Romans considered the law of succession to be part of the law of things, *ius quod ad res pertinet*, since it was thought that succession was a mode of acquiring ownership, namely an *acquisitio per universitatem*, the acquisition of an estate. Since the heir in Roman law not only acquired the property of the deceased, but also took on his debts (plus the fact that the law of succession is closely related to family law), the law of succession should be treated as a separate section of private law.

The Twelve Tables already knew intestate as well as testate succession. The law of intestate succession consisted of the law which determined who would be heir, when a deceased person died without a valid will.

The law of testamentary succession consisted of the rules whereby a testator could by a will himself determine the devolution of his estate after his death.

1. Intestate succession

Intestate succession took place whenever there was no valid will or the instituted heir did not inherit, for whatever reason. The Twelve Tables established the first order of succession on intestacy.

SUI HEREDES

In the first instance, *sui heredes* were entitled to the estate. *Sui heredes* were all persons who were *in potestate* of the deceased and who became *sui iuris* on his death. These were members of his *familia* and the degree of their agnatic relationship to the deceased was irrelevant. The *sui heredes* had to inherit whether they wanted to or not and were, therefore, called *heredes sui et necessarii*.

PROXIMI AGNATI

Secondly, if there were no *sui heredes*, the estate went to the *proximi agnati*, the nearest agnatic relations. The agnates of the nearest degree excluded those who were further removed. In the event of there being several agnates of the same degree, the estate was divided *per capita*, i.e. each of them took an equal share, since there was no *representatio*, representation *per stirpes*, as remoter degrees were excluded. The *proximi agnati* were *heredes voluntarii*, i.e. they could refuse succession.

GENS

If there were no *proximi agnati* the estate devolved on the *gentiles*, the clan.

The main defects of this system were that emancipated children, blood relations and the *sui iuris* spouse were excluded from the estate, since this order of succession was exclusively based on *agnatio*. It is, therefore, not surprising that the *praetor* took steps to improve the system.

2. Praetorian intestate succession

By way of a series of edicts the *praetor* gradually developed a new system of intestate succession, which finally replaced the old order of the *ius civile*.

The complications of his doing so, are summed up in the maxim *'praetor heredem facere non potest'*, the *praetor* could not declare a person *heres*, i.e. heir according to the *ius civile*, because he was no legislator. Nevertheless, in a number of edicts he promised to grant several groups of persons *bonorum possessio*, possession of the inheritance, on application and to protect their possession. This means that the interested party had to approach the *praetor* and apply for *bonorum possessio*. The *praetor* investigated whether the applicant belonged to one of the groups to which *bonorum possessio* was promised and, if this was the case, granted the *interdictum quorum bonorum*.

With this interdict possession of the assets of the estate could be claimed from anyone and once in possession, *usucapio* of one year made the possessor *heres*.

This shows that although the *praetor* could not make anybody *heres*, he could place him in the position of an heir and the end result was thus the same.

The order and groups of praetorian intestate heirs were as follows.

LIBERI

The first group of persons who could claim possession were the *liberi*, the legitimate children of a male deceased, irrespective whether they became *sui iuris* on his death or not. The aim of the relevant edict was to enable emancipated children to inherit from their father. The estate was divided into as many equal portions as there were surviving and predeceased children who left descendants. Each surviving child took one share and the share of the predeceased child was divided among his children. This is known as *representatio per stirpes*.

LEGITIMI

Where there were no *liberi* or they did not apply for *bonorum possessio*, the second group were the *legitimi*, the heirs according to the *ius civile*, i.e. *sui heredes, proximi agnati, gentiles*.

PROXIMI COGNATI

The third group who could request possession in default of all the above relatives, were the *proximi cognati*, the nearest blood relations of the deceased. Blood relationship follows the male as well as the female line in contrast to *agnatio* which followed only the male line. With regard to blood relationship through the female line it was irrelevant whether the descendancy was legitimate or illegitimate.

This was the first time that *cognatio* received recognition in the Roman law of succession. The cognates of the nearest degree excluded those who were further removed. If there were more than one cognate of the same degree, the estate was divided *per capita*, i.e. each of them took an equal share, since there was no *representatio*, representation *per stirpes*, as remoter degrees were excluded. Cognates to the sixth degree could apply under this edict.

VIR ET UXOR

Finally, the surviving spouse could apply for *bonorum possessio*, in terms of the *edictum unde vir et uxor*. This would only apply in case of a marriage *sine manu* where both spouses were *sui iuris*.

In default of all the abovementioned groups, the inheritance became *bona vacantia*, property without an owner and devolved on the state.

The praetorian system remained the basis of intestate succession until Justinian's reforms.

Certain modifications were, however, introduced during the principate to ameliorate the succession of mother and child to one another. During the reign of Hadrian (117-138 AD) the *Senatus Consultum Tertullianum* improved the successory position of the mother with regard to the inheritance of her child. The *Senatus Consultum Orfitianum* called te children first to succeed to thc estate of their mother.

3. Justinian's intestate succession

Justinian introduced in *Novellae* 118 and 127 a completely new order of intestate succession based on blood relationship.

The order and classes of the Justinian system are summarized as follows:

The first class included the *descendentes*, descendants of the deceased, inherited *per stirpes* with *representatio*.

Failing descendants, the estate devolved on the second group, *adscendentes*, ascendants, and brothers and sisters of the deceased.

If there were no members of the second group, half-brothers and half-sisters inherited *per capita*. Failing them, all other blood relations had a turn. Finally, the surviving spouse could succeed. If the deceased left no intestate heirs, the estate went as *bona vacantia* to the *fiscus*, treasury.

4. Testamentary succession

A deceased's estate devolved by intestate succession if there was no valid will, but the testator could choose his own successor(s) by making a will. The law of testate succession laid down the rules relating to the making of a valid will, what dispositions could be made in a will and what effect these dispositions had.

5. Will

The will or *testamentum* was a *testatio mentis*, a declaration of the last will. To be legally valid this declaration of the last will had to be made according to certain formal requirements. During the history of Roman law various forms of wills were known.

The earliest form of will was the so-called *testamentum calatis comitiis*, a will made in the *comitia calata*, a special gathering of the assembly. The testator expressed orally in a formal manner his last will in the assembly. Originally, the assembly had to grant its approval, but later served as witnesses. Since the assembly only met twice a year in the form of the *comitia calata*, it is obvious that another method of will-making was needed. This was the *testamentum in procinctu*, the will made in battle order. The soldier orally declared his last will to the other soldiers.

The disadvantages of these wills are obvious and a third form of *testamentum* thus made its appearance rather soon, i.e. the *testamentum per aes et libram*. This will was made by way of *mancipatio*. In due course it became customary to write down the last will of the testator to serve as proof and to keep the contents of the will secret. This opened the way for the praetorian will.

The *praetor* promised *bonorum possessio*, in other words recognized a will, if a document sealed by seven witnesses, was produced to him.

Finally, the *testamentum tripertitum*, tripartite will, was introduced during the dominate and this was the principal form of will in Justinian's time. The name indicates that this written will consisted of three elements, which had been derived from three sources. The will must be made without interruption, which requirement came from the *ius civile*. Secondly, seven witnesses had to seal the will, which element came from the *ius honorarium*. Finally, the testator and the witnesses had to sign the will, which requirement was derived from imperial legislation. In addition to these normal forms of will, there existed a wide variety of special wills.

6. Codicil

Since Augustus' time (27 BC-14 AD) it was possible to express one's last wishes not only in a will but also in an informal document, a so-called *codicillus*. However, not all dispositions which could be made in a will could be entered into a codicil. The distinction between the *codicillus testamento confirmatus*, a codicil confirmed in a will, and the *codicillus testamento non confirmatus*, the independent codicil, played an important role in this regard. In the former codicil any disposition which could be made in a will, except for the institution of an heir and the disinheritance, could be effected while in the latter codicil only *fideicommissa* could be created.

Justinian assimilated legacies and *fideicommissa*, with the result that legacies could also be left in a *codicillus testamento non confirmatus*.

In post-classical law certain formal requirements were imposed upon codicils and Justinian required five witnesses.

7. Testamenti factio

Testamenti factio activa was the legal capacity to make a valid Roman will.

Originally, only male Roman citizens could do so, but in later law foreigners with *ius commercii* and since Augustus' time women could also make a valid will. The testator had to be over the age of puberty and of sound mind.

Finally, the testator had to be *sui iuris*, since a person without an estate could not make a will. In later law certain exceptions were made regarding the *peculium castrense* and *quasi castrense* of the *filiusfamilias*. In principle the testator had to have *testamenti factio activa* at the time of making his will and retain it without interruption until his death, but there were certain exceptions.

Testamenti factio passiva was the legal capacity to receive under a will.

In principle, any person was eligible, citizens and slaves, over or under the age of puberty, *sui iuris* and *alieni iuris*, sane or insane, all could be heir or legatee.

When a testator instituted his own slave as heir, the slave became free and had to inherit, but if the slave of another was instituted heir, that slave could only accept on the instruction of his owner and the latter acquired the inheritance. Similarly, *alieni iuris* persons, *impubes* and persons under curatorship could only accept an inheritance with the assistance of their *pater*, tutor or curator, or these persons had to accept on their behalf.

At one stage the *testamenti factio passiva* of women was limited, but this limitation fell into disuse. *Personae incertae*, uncertain persons, had no *testamenti factio passiva*. Originally, this meant that legal persons like the state, municipalities, the church and societies could not be instituted as heir or legatee, nor could persons not yet born at the time of the making of the will.

This led to complications in respect of *postumi*, children born after their father's death. Eventually the abovementioned problems were solved by modification of the ban on the institution of *incertae personae*.

Finally some people could forfeit their *testamenti factio passiva* as the result of penal provisions.

Testamenti factio passiva had to exist at the time when the will was made and when it took effect, but not without interruption.

Testamenti factio relativa was the capacity to witness a will. In principle, anybody who had *testamenti factio activa* could be a witness to a will, but some persons were excluded as the result of penalties and others because they had an interest in the will.

8. Contents of the will

In his will the testator disposed of his estate. There was virtually no limit to the variety of dispositions which could be made in a will. The most important part of any will was the institution of the heir which was the essence of a will. Other dispositions generally made in a will were legacies, *fideicommissa*, freeing of slaves and appointment of tutors.

9. Heredis institutio

Heredis institutio was the institution of the heir or heirs. This was an essential requirement for a valid will, since the objective of a will was to exclude intestate succession and thus the will had the primary function of designating the chosen heir or heirs.

Originally the institution of the heir had to be made by formal words and had to be at the head of the will, but in post-classical law the formalism disappeared and any words could be used, as long as the intention of the testator appeared clearly.

The heir in Roman law was a successor *titulo universali*, under universal title, which means that the heir was placed in the patrimonial position of the testator; he succeeded to the patrimonial rights and duties of the deceased, since he inherited the estate, both assets and liabilities.

The testator could institute one heir for the whole estate or several heirs. In the latter case they received equal shares, unless the testator had expressly allotted the amount which each heir was to get.

The testator had to dispose of the whole inheritance, since *'nemo pro parte testatus, pro parte intestatus decedere potest'*, nobody can die partly testate, and partly intestate. Thus, if the testator had disposed of only part of his estate, or if one of the instituted heirs could not or did not want to inherit, the remaining portion of the estate accrued to the heirs who inherited in proportion to their shares. The institution of the heir could be *pure*, unconditionally, or subject to a suspensive condition or a suspensive term or a *modus*. But an institution of an heir subject to a resolutive condition or term was contrary to the rule *'semel heres, semper heres'*, once an heir, he never ceased to be heir, and thus such conditions or terms were treated as *pro non scripto*, not written.

10. Substitutio

Substitutio, substitution, was the appointment of an heir in the place of an instituted heir.

The testator made provision for the possibility that his estate would not devolve upon his chosen heir because the latter could not or would not inherit. This would mean that the will would have no effect and that intestate succession would become operative. Therefore, the testator did not only institute an heir, but made several substitutions, in other words appointed substitute heirs for the eventuality that the instituted heir did not inherit.

Roman law knew three forms of substitution.

Firstly, there was the *substitutio vulgaris*, the normal substitution. To prevent the possibility of his dying intestate, the testator appointed several substitute heirs in his will, ending with one of his slaves. The slave was a *heres necessarius* and thus could not refuse the inheritance. This substitution was thus a conditional institution.

Secondly, the *substitutio pupillaris*, the pupillary substitution was possible. The *paterfamilias* instituted his child under his *potestas* and under the age of puberty, as heir in his will. To make provision for the possibility that the child, after succeeding him, would die before reaching the age of puberty, the father further provided who was to succeed in that case. In effect there were two wills, the one of the *pater* and the second one the *pater* made on the strength of his *potestas* for the *impubes*, who himself could not make a will.

Finally, the *substitutio quasi-pupillaris*, the quasi-pupillary substitution, introduced by Justinian on the model of the *substitutio pupillaris*. Ascendants instituting insane descendants could make wills for these descendants. The choice of substitutes was, however, limited to descendants or brothers and sisters of the lunatic. The underlying idea was also that the lunatic could not himself make a will and, therefore, this was done for him by an ascendant.

11. Legacy

A legacy is a disposition whereby the testator left one or more specific objects to a person. That person, the *legatarius*, legatee, benefitted *titulo singulari*, under special title, which means that he only acquired certain specific things. Originally, legacies had to be made in a will by the use of strict formules, but in later law legacies could also be made in a codicil confirmed by a will and in Justinian's time even in codicils not confirmed by a will. The use of special formal words fell into disuse early in the classical period; any words could be used if the testator's intent was clear. In early Roman law there were four types of legacy, the *legatum per vindicationem, legatum per damnationem, legatum sinendi modi* and the *legatum per praeceptionem*. Each one had its own special form, application and effects. The *Senatus Consultum Neronianum* of the first century AD, provided that where a testator had used the wrong form, it should be construed as if the correct form had been used. This *Senatus Consultum* thus, made the various forms superfluous and Constantine finally abolished them.

OBJECT OF LEGACY

Virtually anything could be the object of a legacy, as long as it was *in commercio*. The testator did not have to be the owner of the object of the legacy, but could bequeath property which belonged to a third person, in which case it is the duty of the heir to buy the property from the owner and to transfer it to the legatee or, if he failed to do so, to pay the legatee the value. If the object of the legacy was, however, already the property of the legatee, the legacy was void.

The legacy was a disposition at the expense of the testate heir. This meant, in the first instance, that the legacy depended upon the coming into effect of the will; in other words if the will for some reason, did not become operative the legacies took no effect either. Secondly, the right of the legatee did not come into being before the instituted heir accepted the inheritance.

VESTING OF LEGACIES

The right of the legatee against the heir arose as soon as the heir accepted the inheritance. Thus, the distinction between the *heres necessarius* and the *heres voluntarius* played an important role. The *heres necessarius*, i.e. the *sui heredes* and slaves of the testator, had to inherit and this means that the will became effective immediately at the *delatio hereditatis*, the falling open of the inheritance. In principle, *delatio hereditatis* took place upon the death of the testator and the right of the legatee became operative immediately.

The *heres voluntarius* or *extraneus* had to accept in order to become heir. Since considerable time could lapse before the heir made up his mind whether to accept or not, and the legatee had in principle no right until the heir had accepted, the jurists developed the doctrine of the *dies legati cedens* and the *dies veniens* to ensure that the legatee would not forfeit his legacy, should he himself die before acceptance by the heir. The *dies cedens legati* was the day of the death of the testator, on which moment the legatee obtained a transmissible expectancy of a right, which right became enforceable on the *dies veniens*, the day of the acceptance of the inheritance by the heir. The legatee was entitled to all accretions since the *dies cedens*, but also bore the risk from that day on.

LAPSE OF LEGACIES

Legacies could be revocated by the testator in a will or a codicil. If the object of the legacy was destroyed, if the institution of an heir did not take effect, if the legatee died before the *dies cedens* or repudiated the legacy, the legatee received nothing.

RESTRICTIONS ON LEGACIES

The Twelve Tables provided that a testator could bequeath as many legacies as he wished in his will and could in fact dispose of all his assets by means of legacies.

This would, however, result in a situation where the heir would refuse to accept the inheritance. It would devolve on intestacy and the legatees would receive nothing.

As a result, a *lex Furia testamentaria* and a *lex Voconia* attempted to restrict the generosity of the testator at the expense of the heir, but this legislation was not very successful. Eventually in 40 BC the *lex Falcidia* was introduced, which finally and effectively settled the matter. The *lex Falcidia* provided that legacies were not to exceed three-quarters of the estate. This entitled the heir to a minimum of one-quarter of the estate, the *quarta Falcidia*.

If the legacies exceeded three-quarters of the estate, they were proportionally decreased. The *quarta Falcidia* was calculated by deduction of the debts, funeral expenses and the value of freed slaves from the value of the estate as at the death. Justinian introduced in his *Novellae* the provision that the testator could expressly exclude the *lex Falcidia* in his will. Justinian moreover, provided that an heir who wanted to invoke the *lex Falcidia* had to make an inventory.

REMEDIES OF THE LEGATEE

Originally, the legal remedy of the legatee depended on the type of legacy. According to Justinian law the legatee had the following actions available to him: (a) the *reivindicatio* where the testator had been the owner of the object of the legacy, (b) the *actio ex testamento*, a personal action against the heir, and (c) the *actio hypothecaria*, since the legatee had a tacit hypothec over the inheritance and the estate of the heir as security for the disbursement of the legacy.

12. Fideicommissum

A *fideicommissum* is a disposition whereby a testator made a request to one person, the *fiduciarius*, to pass a benefit from the estate to another person, the *fideicommissarius*. The origin of *fideicommissa* in Roman law must be attributed to attempts at evading certain restrictions in the law of succession, for example to benefit persons who did not have *testamenti factio passiva* or to evade the *lex Falcidia*.

The testator included an informal request in his will or in a codicil directed at a person who received a benefit from the inheritance, i.e. a testate or intestate heir, legatee or *fideicommissarius*. There was no specific formula for such a request, but the commonly used words were *'fidei tuae committo'*, thus *fideicommissum*.

Initially, the *fideicommissum* placed only a moral duty on the *fiduciarius*, but Augustus decreed that they were enforceable. The request in a *fideicommissum* could be twofold. The testator could request the heir to transfer the whole estate, or part thereof, to the *fideicommissarius*, or he could request that the *fiduciarius* transfer one or more specific assets of the estate to the *fideicommissarius*. The *fideicommissum* could thus be used either instead of the institution of the heir or in the place of a legacy. Thus, Roman law knew two types of *fideicommissa*, the *fideicommissum hereditatis*, the *fideicommissum* of a whole estate or a portion thereof, which showed an increasing resemblance to the institution of the heir, and the *fideicommissum rerum singularum*, the *fideicommissum* of one or more assets of the estate, which approximated the legacy. Justinian equated these two types of dispositions.

OBJECT OF THE FIDEICOMMISSUM

Virtually anything including a whole estate, could be the object of a *fideicommissum* as long as it was *in commercio*.

VESTING AND LAPSE OF FIDEICOMMISSA

In this respect the same principles relating to legacies, applied to *fideicommissa*.

FIDEICOMMISSUM HEREDITATIS

This was a request made to the heir to transfer the whole estate, or part thereof, to the *fideicommissarius*. Several problems arose with regard to such *fideicommissa*. In the first instance, the heir was in fact no more than an intermediary who received no benefits from the inheritance. He might, therefore, be reluctant to accept the inheritance, with the result that the estate would devolve on intestacy. Secondly, if the heir did accept the inheritance he had to transfer the assets, but remained in accordance with the *semel heres, semper heres* rule responsible for the liabilities. For this reason the *Senatus*

Consultum Trebellianum was introduced in approximately 56 AD. It placed the *fideicommissarius heredis loco*, in the position of an heir. Thus, the fideicommissary could be directly sued and could bring actions in respect of the inheritance, *pro rata* to his share in the estate. In short this *Senatus Consultum* solved the problem caused by the *semel heres, semper heres* rule.

The *Senatus Consultum Pegasianum* of approximately 73 AD solved the problem of the heir who refused to accept the inheritance, by providing that the heir was entitled to the *quarta Falcidia* and could be obliged to accept. The complicated legal position which arose where both *Senatus Consulta* were applicable, was solved only by Justinian.

REMEDIES OF THE FIDEICOMMISSARY IN JUSTINIAN LAW

Since Justinian provided that there should be no difference between legacies and *fideicommissa*, the fideicommissary had the *rei vindicatio, actio ex testamento* and the *actio hypothecaria* available to him.

13. Invalidity and revocation of wills

A valid will could become invalid through *capitis deminutio* of the testator if the instituted heir could not, or would not, accept, and by the birth of a *postumus suus*.

Another source of inefficacy of a will was revocation. Since a will contains the last wishes of the testator, it is obvious that a will can be revoked until the death of the testator.

According to the *ius civile* revocation of the will *per aes et libram* could be effected only by the making of a new will. This meant that for every alteration a new will had to be made. In later law, changes which did not relate to the institution of the heir could be made by means of *codicilli testamento confirmati*.

If a testator made a new will, the previous will was automatically ineffective, even if it was not explicitly revoked. Destruction of the document had the effect of invalidating the praetorian will.

14. Limitations on freedom to testate

The *sui heredes* not only had to inherit, but also had the right to inherit. In consequence, a testator who wanted by a will to deviate from the intestate succession, had to expressly disinherit his *sui heredes*. If he neglected to do so the will was void and the estate devolved according to the rules of intestacy.

This means, that although a *pater* could disinherit his *sui heredes* for no reason, the disherison had to be done expressly in a formal manner. The rules of *exheredatio*, disherison, were complicated and underwent considerable change, until Justinian simplified this matter. He provided that all *adscendentes*, ascendants, and *descendentes*, descendants, had to be disinherited *nominatim*, by name, and could only be disinherited, if there was a valid ground to do so.

The second requirement derived from the *querella inofficiosi testamenti*, the material restriction on disherison, which institution was amalgamated by Justinian in his *Novellae* with the *exheredatio*, i.e. the formalities of disherison.

QUERELLA INOFFICIOSI TESTAMENTI

Originally, a testator could freely dispose of his estate and could disinherit his closest kin, as long as he observed the formalities of *exheredatio*. At the end of the republic his freedom of testation was, however, limited by the *querella inofficiosi testamenti*, the complaint of the unduteous will. The underlying principle was that it was unfair and unduteous to favour outsiders at the expense of one's own family in the direct line. These members of the family could by means of the *querella* challenge the will in a special court. When there was no good reason for the disherison, the court declared the will void on the basis of the fiction that the testator must have been insane.

WHO COULD INSTITUTE THE QUERELLA?

Originally, the persons entitled to bring the *querella* were descendants and ascendants of the testator. In late-classical law brothers and sisters of the testator could also bring the *querella*, if *turpes personae*, base persons, had been instituted as heirs.

WHEN COULD THE QUERELLA BE INSTITUTED?

At first the *querella* could only be brought if the family members in question had been disinherited without good cause. In classical law, they could also institute the *querella* if they had been given very little in the will and the rule developed that they could bring the *querella* if they had been left less than a quarter of what they would have received on intestacy. This means that the view had developed that certain persons had a right to a portion of what they would have received on intestacy, the so-called *portio legitima*, which the testator could not deny them by making a will.

EFFECT OF THE QUERELLA

Originally, the whole will was declared null and void and the estate devolved in terms of the law of inteste succession. In post-classical law the tendency developed to keep the will effective as far as possible.

Justinian ruled as follows: If a person entitled to a *portio legitima* had been disinherited without good cause, the institution of the heir fell away and the successful claimant received his intestate share of the estate. The rest of the will, legacies, *fideicommissa*, appointment of tutors, etc. remained valid.

If a person entitled to a *portio legitima* received less, the whole will remained valid, but he could get his share by instituting the *actio ad supplendam legitimam*.

Justinian fixed the *portio legitima* at a third of the intestate portion where a testator left up to four children, and a half of the intestate portion where there were more children. Moreover, he specified a number of good reasons for disherison and thus brought an end to the uncertain casuistry.

15. Obtaining of the inheritance

The vesting of the inheritance depended upon the category of heir, namely the *heres necessarius* or the *heres voluntarius*.

The *heres necessarius*, i.e. the *sui heredes* and own slaves, had no power to refuse the estate and thus the estate vested in him automatically at the *delatio hereditatis*, the falling open of the inheritance, irrespective of whether the estate devolved in terms of the testate or intestate law of succession.

Delatio herditatis occurred, in principle, at the death of the testator.

The *praetor*, later granted *sui heredes* the *ius abstinendi*, the right to abstain from the inheritance. The *heres extraneus* or *voluntarius* first had to accept before they became heir. This means that there were two moments, namely the moment of the *delatio hereditatis* and the moment of the *aditio hereditatis*.

Originally, the acceptance of the inheritance had to be made by a formal declaration, *cretio*, but later this could be done informally by *pro herede gestio*, acting as an heir.

The disadvantages of the informal acceptance, were that it was easily open to doubt whether or not the heir had accepted and there was no period within which the heir was to accept. The second problem could create problems, since the estate was until acceptance a *hereditas iacens*, an estate without owner. The creditors had no one to claim from and the substitute heir and the intestate heirs had no certainty about their position. The heir would delay acceptance since it was irrevocable and he would like to determine whether the estate was solvent or not. To prevent endless delay of acceptance there was *usucapio pro herede*, by means of which anybody could become *heres* of a *hereditas iacens* after taking possession and *usucapio* of one year. Furthermore, the creditors of the estate could bring the heir before the *praetor* and ask him whether he was the heir or not. The *praetor* then determined a period within which the heir must decide to accept or refuse, the *spatium deliberandi*, the period to deliberate, usually one hundred days.

16. Separation of estates of deceased and heir

Once succession had taken place, the estate of the heir and that of the deceased were fused. This could lead to unpleasant results for the creditors of both the deceased and the heir, and for the heir himself, when one of the two estates was insolvent. Consequently measures developed to keep the two estates separate.

SEPARATIO BONORUM

Separatio bonorum, separation of the estates, was introduced by the *praetor* to safeguard the interests of the creditors of the deceased. They could approach the *praetor* and apply for *separatio bonorum*. The *praetor* ordered that the two estates be kept separate until their respective claims had been met. Thus, the deceased's estate was reserved for the creditors of the deceased, who could not claim against the estate of the heir. The inheritance was sold and the creditors of the deceased were paid out of the proceeds; the residue went to the heir. *Separatio bonorum* had to be applied for within five years from acceptance.

BENEFICIUM INVENTARII

Beneficium inventarii, the benefit of making an inventory, was introduced by Justinian to protect the heir. He was entitled to make an inventory of the estate within thirty days of learning of the inheritance. The inventory had to be completed in sixty days from that date. If the heir chose to make use of this benefit, his liability for the debts of the inheritance would have been limited to the amount of the assets of the inheritance. This meant that the two estates were not kept separate, but that the value of the assets of the inheritance was calculated and the heir was liable to this amount with both his own and the inheritance's assets.

17. Co-heirs

Co-heirs became co-owners of the inheritance and could institute the *actio familiae erciscundae* to divide the corporeal assets of the estate. The claims in favour of and against the estate were divided *ipso iure*, automatically, between the co-heirs.

In the calculation of the shares assets were brought into account which did not belong to the actual inheritance, but had to be brought in by the heirs.

COLLATIO BONORUM

Collatio bonorum, bringing in of assets, was introduced by the *praetor* as a result of the *Edictum unde liberi*. In terms of this edict the emancipated child could apply for *bonorum possessio* and thus inherit with the *sui heredes* on intestacy from the *pater*. It would have been unfair towards the *sui heredes* to divide the estate equally among them, since everything the *sui heredes* had acquired during the *pater's* lifetime, was acquired by the *pater*. The *emancipatus*, on the other hand, had often received his *peculium* on emancipation and had been able to acquire property since emancipation. Therefore, the *praetor* decreed that *bonorum possessio* would only be granted to an emancipated child if the latter was prepared to bring in his whole estate into the inheritance. The values of both estates were added and the shares of each heir were calculated, with the result that the *emancipatus* received his share minus his own estate.

Collatio dotis, bringing in of a dowry, was based on the same principle, namely that the *pater* wanted to treat all his descendants equally and that in consequence the descendants had to bring in whatever they had received from the deceased until his death.

18. Remedies of the heir

The principal action available to the heir was the *hereditatis petitio*, an action *in rem* from the *ius civile* which protected the *heres*, the heir according to the *ius civile*. The heir claimed with the *hereditatis petitio* the whole or any part of the inheritance which was possessed by another, irrespective whether the possessor was *bona* or *mala fide*.

The *Senatus Consultum Iuventianum* of the first half of the second century AD, regulated in liability of the *bona fide* and *mala fide* possessor in respect of fruits, damages and expenses on the same lines as the rules with regard to the *causa rei* and the *rei vindicatio*.

INTERDICTUM QUORUM BONORUM

Since the praetorian heir was not *heres*, the *hereditatis petitio* was not available to him. The *praetor* granted the *interdictum quorum bonorum* to recover the whole or any part of the inheritance which was possessed by another, irrespective of whether the possessor was *bona fide* or *mala fide*.

In post-classical and Justinianic law, the distinction between a *heres* and a praetorian heir disappeared, with the result that any heir had both remedies available to him.

BIBLIOGRAPHICAL NOTE

For anyone who wishes to acquire more knowledge of Roman law, there follow a few references which may serve as a starting point.

There exist an enormous number of textbooks on Roman law in the principal modern languages. It would be unwise to attempt to grade these works, but the following books have proved themselves useful:

M. Kaser, Das römische Privatrecht, Erster Abschnitt, München 1971, Zweiter Abschnitt, München 1975;

M. Kaser, Das römische Zivilprozessrecht, München 1966;

J.C. van Oven, Leerboek van romeinsch privaatrecht, Leiden 1948;

W.W. Buckland, A Text-book of Roman Law from Augustus to Justinian (3rd ed revised by P. Stein), Cambridge 1966;

P.F. Girard, Manuel élémentaire de droit romain (8 ème ed par F. Senn), Paris 1929;

R. Monier, Manuel élémentaire de droit romain, tome I, Paris 1947; tome II, Paris 1954;

P. Bonfante, Corso di diritto romano, (4 vol) Rome 1925-1930;

B. Biondi, Istituzioni di diritto romano, Milano 1972;

The most important literature is, however, the Roman law texts, the so-called sources. The most important of these is the *Corpus Iuris Civilis.* The edition usually consulted is that of Mommsen, Krüger, Schöll, Kroll.

Another source to consult are the *Institutiones* of Gaius and the edition useful for english-speaking readers is that of De Zulueta.

Most other sources are included in *Fontes iuris romani anteiustiniani* by Riccobono, Baviera, Furlani, Arangio-Ruiz.

Finally, there are the articles on Roman law in specialized legal journals. In this respect the publications of the Centre de Documentation des droits antiques are extremely valuable, in that it publishes a list of all literature published during a year as well as a key-word register on, amongst others, Roman law.

www.ingramcontent.com/pod-product-compliance
Lightning Source LLC
LaVergne TN
LVHW011133300926
849160LV00008B/635